P-47 THUNDERBOLT
VS
Bf 109G/K

Europe 1943–45

MARTIN BOWMAN

First published in Great Britain in 2008 by Osprey Publishing,
Midland House, West Way, Botley, Oxford, OX2 0PH, UK
443 Park Avenue South, New York, NY 10016, USA

E-mail: info@ospreypublishing.com

A CIP catalog record for this book is available from the British Library

ISBN: 978 1 84603 315 5

Edited by Tony Holmes
Cockpit and gunsight artwork by Jim Laurier
Cover artwork and battlescene by Gareth Hector
Three-views and armament scrap views by Chris Davey
Page layout by Myriam Bell Design, France
Index by Alan Thatcher
Typeset in ITC Conduit and Adobe Garamond
Maps by Boundford.com, Huntingdon, UK
Originated by PDQ Digital Media Solutions
Printed and bound in China through Bookbuilders

08 09 10 11 12   10 9 8 7 6 5 4 3 2 1

FOR A CATALOG OF ALL BOOKS PUBLISHED BY OSPREY MILITARY AND
AVIATION PLEASE CONTACT:

NORTH AMERICA
Osprey Direct, c/o Random House Distribution Center, 400 Hahn Road,
Westminster, MD 21157

E-mail: info@ospreydirect.com

ALL OTHER REGIONS
Osprey Direct UK, P.O. Box 140 Wellingborough, Northants, NN8 2FA, UK

E-mail: info@ospreydirect.co.uk

Osprey Publishing is supporting the Woodland Trust, the UK's leading woodland
conservation charity, by funding the dedication of trees.

www.ospreypublishing.com

Acknowledgments:

Photographs for this volume have been supplied from the archives of Martin Bowman, Eddie
Creek, Jerry Scutts, John Weal and the late Roger Freeman.

P-47D cover art
Maj Kenneth Gallup, commanding officer of the 353rd
FG's 350th FS, plunges headlong into a formation of
30+ Bf 109Gs from III./JG 53 at 1315hrs north of the
German town of Soltau on August 4, 1944. Gallup was
flying his assigned P-47D-25 42-26634 at the time,
having "made ace" in this machine four weeks earlier.
His squadron was defending some 320 B-17s sent to
bomb the Hamburg oil refinery when it was bounced
by the "Gustavs" of III./JG 53, the latter attacking
the Thunderbolts at a height of 30,000ft. The entry in the
353rd FG's combat diary for August 4 noted that "at
approximately 1315hrs, ten miles north of Soltau, the
350th FS, led by Maj Gallup, reported being bounced by
30+ Me 109s. The fierce fight which ensued broke the
squadron up, with some pilots following enemy aircraft
down to the deck while others hunted in the cumulus
cloud. Group leader Gallup claimed 2 Me 109s destroyed,
but one had to be reduced to a probable." Kenneth Gallup
finished his combat tour with nine victories (including
seven Bf 109s) to his credit, all of them claimed whilst
flying the P-47D. (Artwork by Gareth Hector)

Bf 109K-4 cover art
In the final months of the war in Europe, most aerial
clashes between P-47s and Bf 109s saw Defence of the
Reich fighters engaging Ninth Air Force Thunderbolts
attacking ground targets. One such clash took place
during the early afternoon of February 19, 1945, when
13 Bf 109K-4s of 11./JG 53 and eight Fw 190As from
an unknown Geschwader bounced 16 P-47D-30s of the
362nd FG shortly after the latter had strafed a railway
marshalling yard at Westerburg, in southwestern Germany.
Leading the aircraft from 11./JG 53 was Staffelkäpitan
Leutnant Günther Landt, who dived through the
Thunderbolt formation from a height of 16,000ft. Upon
his return to base at Kirrlach, Landt claimed two P-47s
destroyed, thus taking his tally to 18. He would lead
11./JG 53 through to war's end, by which point he
had increased his score to 23 victories (including nine
Thunderbolts). According to official USAAF loss records,
the 362nd FG suffered no casualties on February 19,
1945, with the Thunderbolt pilots in turn claiming three
Bf 109s and three Fw 190s desroyed. The American pilots
also reported that the "German fighters were aggressive,
but seemed inexperienced." (Artwork by Gareth Hector)

CONTENTS

INTRODUCTION

For much of 1942, the defense of the German Reich was entrusted predominantly to Luftwaffe units equipped with the Messerschmitt Bf 109. Pilots of this iconic fighter, along with their brethren flying the equally deadly Focke-Wulf Fw 190, were inflicting increasing losses on the heavy bomber groups of the fledgling Eighth Air Force as the United States Army Air Force (USAAF) attempted to make its presence felt in the European Theater of Operations (ETO). On average, some 13.6 percent of the attacking force sent out to hit targets in western Europe would fall victim to the Jagdwaffe. Such losses could not be allowed to continue, but at the time neither the Royal Air Force (RAF) or the USAAF had a fighter in-theater with sufficient range to protect the vulnerable B-17 Flying Fortresses and B-24 Liberators as they ventured ever deeper into enemy territory.

In late 1942, as a first step in providing the "heavies" with much-needed strategic escorts, 200 Republic P-47C Thunderbolts were shipped to the UK. Although some believed the Lockheed P-38 Lightning to be the better strategic fighter thanks to its twin engines and longer range, demand for it in other theaters meant that the Thunderbolt was the only modern fighter available in sufficient quantity to serve as the principal interceptor for the Eighth Air Force in the short term.

Three groups in VIII Fighter Command were initially equipped with the P-47, and they were declared operational in April 1943. These groups subsequently endured some hard knocks at the hands of battle-seasoned German fighter units, and despite their best efforts, Thunderbolt pilots were initially handicapped by poor tactics and combat inexperience.

One of the P-47's primary tormentors in 1943 was the Bf 109G, which was the most-produced version of the Messerschmitt fighter. Having seen four years of combat in European skies, the German interceptor had been continually modified in order for it to remain a viable fighter in the face of growing Allied aerial opposition.

The Jagdwaffe pilots equipped with Bf 109Gs were, in the main, as "salty" as the aircraft they flew. Their experience was brought to bear throughout 1943 and into early 1944, as the P-47 groups struggled to protect the longer-ranging heavy bombers that were still being brought down in growing numbers by German fighters.

Both the Thunderbolt and the Bf 109G represented astounding advances in fighter engine and armament design, but they could not have been more different. The sleek, aesthetically pleasing Messerschmitt was half the weight of the heavyweight, barrel-shaped, American fighter. Indeed, the Thunderbolt was the largest and heaviest single-engined single-seat propeller-driven fighter ever built. It climbed like a homesick angel and dived for the deck like a rock. This was due to the mighty power of its air-cooled, turbosupercharged Pratt & Whitney R-2800 Double Wasp engine. Pilots disparagingly dubbed it the "seven-ton milk bottle." Other sobriquets included "the Repulsive Scatterbolt," "Thunderjug" and "Thundermug."

But sheer size was not to prove detrimental to the Thunderbolt's operational career. Indeed, P-47s flew 546,000 combat sorties from March 1943 to August 1945, and only 0.7 percent of them were lost in combat. Yet although the "Jug" could out-dive any other fighter at low and medium altitudes, it could not match the rate of climb or maneuverability of the Bf 109G and later Bf 109K variant. Another shortcoming was insufficient range to permit deep penetration into Germany, and this was only rectified with the introduction of progressively larger wing drop tanks.

P-47 pilots came to typify the might of the Eighth Air Force's fighter strength from the summer of 1943 through to mid-1944, when the P-51 assumed the crown of king of USAAF fighters in the ETO. Nonetheless, while the Mustang became the finest long-range fighter of the war, more Thunderbolts were built than any other US fighter.

Like the P-47, the Bf 109 was eventually usurped as the best piston-engined fighter in Luftwaffe service, with the improved Fw 190 (radial and inline-engined versions) being seen as the better aircraft as the war progressed. However, through sheer weight of numbers, and hasty upgrades, the Bf 109G/K remained a deadly opponent in the hands of combat veterans. Unfortunately for the Jagdwaffe, the latter were in very short supply by the summer of 1944, as so many of its *Experten* had fallen trying to repel the overwhelming Allied aerial onslaught, at the heart of which was the Thunderbolt.

CHRONOLOGY

1933
July 6 Reichsluftfahrtministerium (RLM) issues Tactical Requirements for Fighter Aircraft (Land). The Messerschmitt Bf 109 is one of four designs put forward.

1934
March Design work commences on the Bf 109.

1935
May 28 Rolls-Royce Kestrel-powered Bf 109 V1 prototype successfully performs its maiden flight.

1936
January Junkers Jumo 210-powered Bf 109 V2 joins the flight trial program, where both prototypes are flown alongside the rival Heinkel He 112 fighter.
Autumn Following a series of exhaustive trials, the Bf 109 is eventually chosen for series production ahead of the He 112 due to it being both faster and more maneuverable.

1937
February First example of 344 Bf 109Bs leaves the Augsburg factory and is issued to II./JG 132 "Richthofen."
June Bf 109 V10 fitted with a Daimler-Benz DB 600Aa engine.

1938
Spring Bf 109C, fitted with fuel-injected Jumo 210Ga engine and wing-mounted machine guns, enters production. Bf 109D, powered by the Jumo 210Da engine with a carburetor, also enters series production at the same time.

December First production Bf 109E-1s, fitted with the definitive fuel-injected Daimler-Benz DB 601 engine, enter frontline service. The aircraft's overall performance was drastically improved with the fitment of the new engine.

1939
Sept 1 German troops invade Poland, and Bf 109Cs from I./JG 21 claim five PZL P.24s destroyed as the fighter's first victories of World War II.

1940
Jan 17 Republic XP-47 and XP-47A prototypes approved.
July 10 Bf 109E fitted with DB 601E engine flies and leads to Bf 109F series.
Sept 13 Contract for 171 P-47Bs and 602 P-47Cs placed.

1941
March Bf 109F-1 enters service.
May 6 XP-47B flies for the first time.
Oct 14 Contract for 850 P-47Ds placed.
Dec 21 First of 169 P-47Bs delivered.

Bf 109G-6 "Kanonenboot" Wk.-Nr. 27083 of 5./JG 2 is pushed out onto the concrete dispersal area at Evreux in early October 1943. This aircraft was shot down by 84th FS/78th FG P-47 ace LtCol Eugene Roberts on October 20, 1943.

1942

Jan 31	Contract for 1,050 P-47Ds and 354 P-47Gs placed.
Feb 23	Eighth Air Force arrives in Britain.
March 18	Deliveries of the P-47B begin.
June	First Bf 109G-1/2s begin reaching the Eastern Front.
August 17	First American heavy bomber raid flown from England.
September	P-47B production completed. Evansville, Indiana, plant completes and flies first P-47D.

1943

Jan 27	First USAAF attack on Germany.
February	56th and 78th FGs declared operational on the P-47C/D in England.
February	Bf 109G-6 reaches the front line for the first time, this version subsequently becoming the most-built variant of the Messerschmitt fighter, with 12,000+ delivered by war's end (more than a third of the entire production run for the Bf 109).
March	Bf 109G-3 enters service.
April 13	Inaugural Eighth Air Force P-47 mission flown over Occupied Europe.
May 4	First P-47 bomber escort mission flown.
May 13	First P-47 claimed shot down by a Bf 109G, credited to 78-kill ace Leutnant Georg-Peter Eder of 12./JG 2 (no USAAF losses reported).
May 18	First Bf 109Gs claimed shot down by P-47s, with victories credited to Capt T. J. Andrews and Lt D. W. Beeson (17.333 kills) of the 334th FS/4th FG.
June 22	First deep penetration of Germany, to Hüls, near Recklinghausen, on the edge of the Ruhr.
July 28	56th and 78th FGs carry ferry tanks for the first time.

1944

Jan 1	US Strategic Air Forces in Europe established to control operations of Eighth and Fifteenth Air Forces.
April	P-47D production lines change from the "razorback" shape to the bubble canopy.
June 6	D-Day. Seventeen England-based P-47D groups, 13 of them in the Ninth Air Force, take part.
June 30	1,900 P-47Ns approved.
July 22	XP-47N flies.
October	Bf 109K enters frontline service.

1945

April 7	Last Bf 109 aerial claims made by Eighth Air Force P-47s, with four aircraft being credited to the 56th FG.
April 16	Last Bf 109 aerial claims made by Ninth Air Force P-47s.
April 19	Last P-47s (Ninth Air Force aircraft) claimed shot down by Bf 109s, credited to pilots of III./JG 53.
April 21	Last combat missions flown by Eighth Air Force P-47s.
May 8	Last combat missions flown by Ninth Air Force P-47s
July	Evansville P-47 production ceases.
December	Farmingdale P-47 production ceases.

P-47D-30-RE 44-20571 of the Ninth Air Force's 386th FS/365th FG has its engine run up by its pilot in front of a mobile flak battery at the group's base in Metz, France, in late 1944. The 365th FG began combat operations with the Ninth Air Force in February 1944, moving to France in late June. On January 30, 1945, the group moved to Florennes/Juzaine, in Belgium, remaining there until March 16, when its P-47s were transferred to Aachen, in Germany.

DESIGN AND DEVELOPMENT

P-47 THUNDERBOLT

In June 1940, the United States Army Air Corps (USAAC) issued a requirement for new lightweight fighter designs, and among those manufacturers to respond was the Republic Aviation Corporation of Farmingdale, New York. Although a relatively "new" company, Republic had inherited vast experience in fighter design from its predecessor, the Seversky Aircraft Corporation. Republic's chief engineer, Alexander Kartveli, who, like his former chief, Maj Alexander P. Seversky, was of Russian extraction, had previously designed the P-35 to meet a 1935 USAAC fighter requirement.

Republic had also received contracts in September 1939 for limited production of the P-43 Lancer. This aircraft had good high-altitude performance, but it was deemed to be inferior overall to European fighter types such as the Spitfire and Bf 109E.

Kartveli, meanwhile, had a new fighter project on the drawing board called the AP-10, which was a relatively lightweight machine designed around a 1,150hp Allison V-1710-39 liquid-cooled V12 inline engine and armed with two 0.50-in. machine guns in the nose. The Allison was more powerful and less expensive than the air-cooled Pratt & Whitney R-1830 radial that had powered the Seversky pursuits, and in 1939 the Curtiss XP-40, with its mechanically supercharged Allison V-1710-19 inline engine, had relegated the Seversky fighters to also-rans.

However, the estimated performance of the AP-10, designated the XP-47 (armed with two 0.50-in. nose guns and four 0.30-in. machine guns in the wings) and lightweight XP-47A (two nose guns only) by the USAAC, did not meet with official approval. Kartveli therefore abandoned his inline-engined designs so that he could concentrate all of Republic's resources on the development of a radically different fighter aircraft.

The most powerful engine then available was the huge 2,000hp Pratt & Whitney R-2800-21 Double Wasp 18-cylinder two-row radial. Adapting this massive engine to power a fighter aircraft required a great feat of engineering, but Kartveli and his team knew that without it, their design could not possibly meet the performance and load-carrying demands required of the new fighter by the USAAC. A four-bladed 12ft diameter propeller had to be used to harness the power created by the R-2800, and Kartveli produced an efficient supercharging duct system that offered the least interrupted airflow using the unorthodox method of designing this feature first and then building up the fuselage around it.

The engine's huge turbosupercharger was stowed internally in the rear fuselage, with the large intake for the air duct mounted beneath the powerplant, together with the oil coolers. Exhaust gases were piped back separately from the engine to the turbosupercharger and expelled through a waste gate in the bottom of the fuselage, with ducted air fed to the centrifugal impeller and returned under pressure via an intercooler to the engine.

Kartveli designed a telescopic landing gear that was nine inches shorter when retracted than when extended so as to make room for the wing installation of no fewer than eight 0.5-in. machine guns and their ammunition, which when fired imposed immense loads and stresses on the aircraft that had to be taken into consideration. Last, but not least, the great quantities of fuel necessary to power the 12,086lb beast required internal tanks to hold 307 US gallons of fuel.

P-47C/Ds from the 62nd FS/56th FG form up in echelon down formation for the benefit of the press huddled in a B-24 during a photo flight over Suffolk on May 25, 1943.

Assigned to leading P-47
ace LtCol Francis "Gabby"
Gabreski, P-47D-25 42-26418
was one of the first
"bubbletop" Thunderbolts
issued to the 56th FG in the
ETO. The leading P-47 Bf 109
killer, Gabreski downed at
least four "Gustavs" with this
aircraft in June–July 1944,
taking his final wartime tally
of aerial victories to 28 (11 of
these were Bf 109s). Gabreski
hit the ground in 42-26418
whilst strafing He 111s
at Bassenheim airfield on
July 20, 1944, forcing him
to crash-land. He spent the
rest of the war as a POW.

62nd FS/56th FG P-47D-2
42-22537 was photographed
at a remote dispersal at
Halesworth, in Suffolk, in
early 1944. This aircraft was
the regular mount of Bf 109
killer Maj Leroy A. Schreiber,
who had claimed 12 victories
by the time he was shot down
and killed by flak on April 15,
1944. Schreiber was credited
with the destruction of eight
Bf 109s, 5.5 of which were
claimed in this very P-47.

The XP-47B Thunderbolt prototype was larger than all previous fighters by a substantial margin. Indeed, it was more than twice the weight of most of its contemporaries, yet the powerful radial engine enabled it to reach a maximum speed of 412mph shortly after making its maiden flight on May 6, 1941.

Across the Atlantic, the appearance of another radial-engined fighter in the shape of the BMW 801 powered Focke-Wulf Fw 190 over France just weeks earlier had caused alarm within the ranks of the RAF. In European terms, the P-47 and the Fw 190 were unusual in concept, as the majority of fighter types in frontline service were powered by liquid-cooled inline engines. However, the Fw 190 in particular outperformed all existing types by a wide margin, with its compact radial engine rendering the Focke-Wulf especially effective at low altitude – a trait that the P-47 would also exhibit once it reached the ETO later in the war.

While the Fw 190 cemented its reputation in combat both on the Channel Front and in the east against the Soviet air force in the early months of 1942, production difficulties and numerous technical problems hindered the development of the Thunderbolt. The first of 171 P-47Bs left the Republic plant in March of that year, but it was not until June that the 56th Fighter Group (FG) was issued with the first examples to reach a frontline unit.

From September 1942 production switched to the P-47C, some 602 examples eventually being built. This variant differed from the B-model in having a slightly lengthened (by 10.5in.) forward fuselage, a new engine mounting, changes to the rudder and elevator balance system to improve its flight characteristics and the ability to carry a 200-gal ventral drop-tank. The latter permitted units equipped with the aircraft in England (the 56th and 78th FGs had arrived from the US in January 1943, joining the 4th FG, which would swap its Spitfire VBs for P-47Cs) to fly deep penetrations into Occupied Europe from July 1943.

The P-47C-1 had fixed deflection plates fitted between the oil cooler shutters and the exhaust waste gates, improvements made to its electrical system, undercarriage and brakes, and the addition of a hydraulic flap equalizer. The P-47C-2 differed from

P-47D-25 THUNDERBOLT

36ft 1.75in.

14ft 2in.

226418

HV ★ A

40ft 9.25in.

the C-1 only by being fitted with a metal-covered rudder and elevators. All early-build P-47s left the factory equipped with the Mk VIII reflector gunsight, as well as a simple ring and post sight, as standard. The K-14 gyroscopic gunsight was eventually factory-installed in Thunderbolts from late 1944, although many P-47s in the ETO had had the sight fitted through base- or depot-level modification.

The factory-installed rear view mirror above the windscreen framing was generally considered inadequate for a pilot to see behind him in combat, so P-47 units tried various mirror arrangements. It was not uncommon for some of the fighters to have three mirrors, with additional ones fitted to the sides of the windscreen framing. Others sported two large Spitfire-type mirrors fixed to the top of the windscreen framing. Plexiglas "bubble" panels originally supplied for better observation on bombers were also fitted in place of the side Plexiglas of the P-47's canopy. Such modifications were rendered superfluous with the development of the "bubbletop" P-47D in the spring of 1944, however.

The P-47D-1, of which 114 were built from December 1942, was the first Thunderbolt model produced at the company's new Evansville, Indiana, plant. It differed little from previous models except for the standardization of water injection into the intake manifold to produce more prolonged combat power of 2,300hp at 27,000ft. Other changes included additional armor protection for the pilot, fuel and oxygen system upgrades and the exhaust ducting was again modified for improved reliability and performance. The 114 P-47D-RAs from Evansville were identical to Farmingdale-built P-47C-2-REs. P-47D-1-REs differed from earlier versions in having an additional pair of flaps on the engine cowl to vastly improve cooling of the R-2800-21 engine, which suffered from cylinder head overheating.

Paddle-bladed airscrews of increased diameter were fitted to the D-models as standard, and these helped absorb the full war emergency power of the R-2800-59 engine. One of the first pilots to fly a P-47D fitted with broader chord propellers in the ETO – in early 1944 – was 1Lt Robert S. Johnson of the 56th FG's 61st FS, who would eventually claim 27 kills (nine of which were Bf 109s) in the Thunderbolt. He provided details of his first flight in a modified P-47 in his postwar autobiography, *THUNDERBOLT!*:

New Year's Day, and what a present we received. We flew to a maintenance depot at Wattisham to have the Thunderbolts modified. Our engineering officers were making a terrific fuss over a new propeller designed especially for the Thunderbolt. They insisted that the fat paddle blades of the new propellers would bring a tremendous boost in performance, as the increased blade area would permit the props to make the greatest use of the Thunderbolt's 2,000 horsepower. We listened to their enthusiastic ramblings with more than a grain of salt – and never were we more mistaken. What a difference the blades made when I took my modified fighter up for the first time. It quivered and began to shake badly as if partially stalled. The next thing I knew I was in dive and *wow*! I hauled back on the stick, afraid that the engine would tear right out of the mounts. What I didn't realize was that the new propeller was making all the difference. At 8,000ft I pulled the Thunderbolt into a steep climb. Normally, she'd zoom quickly and then slow down, rapidly approaching a stall. But now the Jug soared up like she'd gone crazy.

Another Thunderbolt was in the air, and I pulled alongside, signaling for a climb. I left that other fighter behind as if he were standing still. The Jug stood on her tail and howled her way into the sky. Never again did an Fw 190 or Me 109 outclimb me in the Thunderbolt. The new propeller was worth 1,000hp, and then some.

According to Johnson's CO, the legendary 17.75-kill ace Col Hubert "Hub" Zemke, the "wide blade propeller took a much bigger bite of air and improved the fighter's rate of climb at low altitudes." The props, when combined with the newly introduced water injection equipment which boosted the engine's performance for short intervals, gave the P-47D a dramatic improvement in its rate of climb by around 600ft per minute. "We could now top 30,000ft in about 13 minutes, instead of 20," Zemke recalled.

The P-47D's top speed of 433mph at 30,000ft and its formidable performance in the dive made it ideal for flying top cover for high-flying B-17 and B-24 heavy bomber formations that eventually reached as far as Berlin from bases in eastern England.

For the fighter-bomber role, the aircraft's "universal" wing and underbelly mountings permitted various combinations of up to 2,500lb of bombs, two 150-gal tanks and one 75-gal tank and, later, rocket projectiles in a tube cluster to be carried. A full bombload meant that ammunition for each of the six or eight 0.50-in. machine guns was reduced from 425 to 267 rounds, but the Thunderbolt's firepower remained undiminished.

During strafing attacks, the weight of the bombload and drop-tanks added to that of the aircraft resulted in a terrific increase in speed when the fighter went into a dive. It could cause a surge or vapor lock in the fuel lines, as the fuel pump was unable to meet the "g" loads imposed, and a number of P-47s suffered engine failure over enemy

P-47D-28 44-19566 of the 78th FG at Duxford in D-Day markings in late June 1944.

territory as a result of this problem. The P-47D-15 was the first Thunderbolt built with underwing pylons and fuel system plumbing within the wings to allow the aircraft to fly with expendable fuel tanks. Internal fuel capacity was also boosted to 375-gal and the overall bombload increased to 2,500lb. Finally, the canopy was made completely jettisonable too.

The "razorback" P-47D was built in numerous sub-variants, ranging from the D-1 up to the D-24, and these differed from one another in respect to their engine specification and wing weapon/plumbing fit.

The first major structural change to the Thunderbolt came with production of the P-47D-25 in late 1943. In July of that year, the last D-5 built was given a cut-down rear fuselage and a clear-view bubble canopy sourced from a British Hawker Typhoon. Designated the XP-47K, the aircraft proved to be so popular with test pilots that the new "blown" Perspex canopy was immediately introduced to the Thunderbolt production line starting with the P-47D-25-RE at Farmingdale and the P-47D-26-RA at Evansville.

Prior to the phasing out of production of the "razorback" Thunderbolt, some 3,962 D-models had been built at Farmingdale and 1,461 at Evansville. From the "Dash 25" onwards, the two plants produced 2,547 and 4,632 D-models. By the time the first of these aircraft – unofficially dubbed "Superbolts" by frontline pilots – reached the ETO, aircraft were being delivered to the USAAF unpainted. The 56th FG received its first P-47D-25s in May 1944, and Col "Hub" Zemke was an early recipient as he recalled in his autobiography *The HUB – Fighter Leader*:

This P-47M from the 56th FG was stripped of its panels and put on display at Boxted on August 1, 1945 as part of the US Army Air Forces Day, which saw the base open its gates to the British public. Hundreds of local boys queued up to take a peek into the cockpit of the big fighter, parked outside Boxted's No. 1 hangar.

The one-piece clear cockpit canopy provided the pilot with excellent all round visibility, and helped cut down the fatigue from neck twisting. The only drawback was that the rear fuselage cockpit fairing had been removed, affecting the directional stability of the aircraft. The other welcome change with the Superbolt was an enlarged internal fuel tank providing an extra 65 gallons. This allowed us to take the maximum advantage of our external tanks, for we could push much farther into Germany and still be able to return on internally held fuel.

By the time production of the P-47D ended with the D-40-RA, which featured a dorsal fin (first installed as a retrofit in the field on the D-27) to cure instability problems that had always afflicted the "bubbletop" Thunderbolt, some 12,602 D-models had been built – the largest production quantity of one sub-type of any US fighter ever produced.

The next P-47 variant to attain series production was the high-speed M-model, hastily built to combat the V1 flying bomb threat in the summer of 1944. The aircraft was essentially a late-build P-47D fitted with a more powerful R-2800-57(C) engine that boasted an uprated CH-5 turbosupercharger, the latter having been trialed in the XP-47J – this machine attained 504mph during flight tests in 1944. The P-47M was also fitted with airbrakes in the wings to help the pilot slow the big fighter down when trying to achieve a firing position behind a slower enemy aircraft.

Just 130 "sprint" P-47Ms were built, and these were used exclusively by the 56th FG from the late summer of 1944. Abnormally low cylinder head temperatures, breakdown of the ignition systems at high altitude and other engine problems dogged P-47M operations, and the group enjoyed only moderate success with the aircraft.

The final variant to attain production was the P-47N, which was significantly different to the ubiquitous D-model. The aircraft was fitted with a new long-span wing tailored to cope with the much-increased weight of the Thunderbolt – it also contained fuel cells for the very first time. The wing, which was 18in. greater in span and boasted 22 sq. ft of extra area, incorporated larger ailerons and square-cut tips that significantly increased the roll rate. The fighter's undercarriage was also strengthened to meet the rise in weight by 750lb to 21,200lb. Large orders were placed for the aircraft, but Farmingdale had completed just 1,667 airframes and Evansville 149 when contracts were canceled in December 1945 in the wake of VE- and VJ-Days.

It was intended that the P-47N would equip the 56th FG, but the war ended before the "Wolf Pack" could get them into combat, and the type was used exclusively in the Pacific theater, where its extended range made the aircraft an excellent strategic bomber escort.

P-47D/Ns remained in USAF service for a number of years after the war, passing to Air National Guard units before being phased out of service in 1955. By then all surviving Thunderbolts had been redesignated F-47D/Ns.

Altogether, 15,683 examples of the Thunderbolt were built. Although not as high a number as for the Bf 109, Spitfire or Yak series of fighters, this figure makes the P-47 the most-produced American fighter of all time.

Bf 109

Undoubtedly the most famous German fighter ever, and built in greater numbers than any other aircraft except for the Ilyushin Il-2, the Messerschmitt Bf 109 fought in the Spanish Civil War and World War II. The aircraft's origins can be traced back to the fledgling Luftwaffe's desire to modernize its fighter force in the early 1930s.

On July 6, 1933, the Reichsluftfahrtministerium (RLM), headed by Hermann Göring, issued Tactical Requirements for Fighter Aircraft (Land). This document stated that the Luftwaffe needed a single-seat daytime fighter armed with two fixed machine guns (1,000 rounds) or one fixed cannon (100 rounds). It had to have a radio for air-to-air and air-to-ground communication, as well as a safety harness, oxygen system, parachute, and heating for the pilot. The fighter had to be able to maintain a speed of 400km/h for up to 20 minutes at 6,000m, possess at least an hour's flight duration and take no longer than 17 minutes to reach this height. Its ultimate ceiling was to be 10,000m.

From a handling perspective, the aircraft had to be capable of diving and turning without losing altitude, and be easily recoverable from a spin. The fighter also had to be operable from the average German airfield, which was 400m x 400m in size, by an average frontline pilot. It would also be required to fly in cloud and fog, and to perform group (up to nine aircraft) take-offs and landings. Finally, the design must be small enough to enable it to be transported by rail.

Having already built fighters for the Luftwaffe, Arado, Heinkel and Focke-Wulf were seen as front runners to win this lucrative contract, and Messerschmitt, which had no experience in designing fighters, was seen as the rank outsider. The company had a long history of aircraft construction, however, having taken over the Udet Flugzeugbau in July 1926. Bayerische Flugzeugwerke AG had merged with fellow aircraft manufacturer Messerschmitt Flugzeugbau at this time, and company founder, Dipl.-Ing. Willy Messerschmitt, assumed design control within the new enterprise.

Its series of fast sports aircraft from the late 1920s and early 1930s, boasting low-set, cantilever wings, gave the RLM the confidence to instruct Messerschmitt to build a four-seater touring aircraft to compete in the 1934 European Flying Contest. The M 23 design by Willy Messerschmitt had won this prestigious international competition in 1929 and 1930, and the new aircraft produced by the company was eventually designated the Bf 108.

Design work on the Bf 109 commenced in secret in March 1934 at the Bayerische Flugzeugwerke AG facility in Augsburg-Haunstetten, in Bavaria. Many features embodied in the Bf 108 would find their way into the Bf 109 prototype, including flush-riveted stressed-skin construction, cantilevered monoplane wings, equipped with Handley Page "slots" along the leading edges, and a narrow track undercarriage attached to the fuselage and retracting outwards into wells forward of the main spar.

Buoyed by the success of the Bf 108, Messerschmitt pressed on with the Bf 109, which incorporated all of the features previously mentioned. Aside from the wing "slots," the aircraft also had trailing edge flaps, and the two combined with the flying surfaces' small surface area (made possible by the growing power of aero engines) to

Bf 109G-5/AS

29ft 7in.

8ft 2.5in.

32ft 6.5in.

ultimately give the Bf 109 unmatched maneuverability. The fuselage itself was made of light metal as a monocoque structure of roughly oval section, constructed in two halves and joined along the centerline.

Right from the start, Messerschmitt had planned that the lightweight Bf 109 would be powered by one of the new generation inverted-Vee 12-cylinder engines under development by Junkers and Daimler-Benz. The former's 680hp Jumo 210 was ultimately selected because it was at a more advanced stage in its development than the 960hp DB 600Aa. As it transpired, delivery of the Junkers powerplant was delayed to the point where the first prototype Bf 109 V1 had to be fitted with a 695hp Rolls-Royce Kestrel VI engine.

Construction of the of the V1 was completed by early May 1935, and following a series of taxiing trials, on the 28th of that month Messerschmitt's senior test pilot, Hans-Dietrich "Bubi" Knoetzsch, made the fighter's first flight from Augsburg-Haunstetten airfield. Following initial factory trials, the aircraft was sent to the Rechlin-based *Erprobungsstelle* (testing center) for service evaluation. The latter soon proved that the Bf 109 was much faster and more maneuverable than its primary rival for the fighter contract, Heinkel's He 112 V1 (which was also Kestrel-powered).

The Jumo 210A-powered Bf 109 V2 took to the skies in October 1935 and joined the trials program three months later. This aircraft also boasted two 7.9mm MG 17 machine guns in the fuselage upper decking. The V3, which had provision for an engine-mounted 20mm MG FF/M cannon firing through the propeller hub, flew for the first time in June 1936, and a short while later both Messerschmitt and Heinkel received contracts from the RLM to build ten pre-production aircraft.

In the autumn of that year the official trials culminated in a series of tests at Travemünde, where the Bf 109 proved its superiority in a memorable flight demonstration that included tailslides, flick rolls, 21-turn spins, tight turns and terminal dives. Being faster in level speed and in the climb than the He 112, and easily able to outdive the Heinkel, the Bf 109 could also perform much tighter turns thanks to its leading-edge slots. From rank outsider, Messerschmitt had become the obvious choice for the contract, and the Bf 109 was duly announced the competition winner.

Production Bf 109Bs entered service in Germany in February 1937, these early aircraft being built at Messerschmitt's Augsburg-Haunstetten plant. It soon became clear that a larger factory would be required, however, so a new site at Regensburg was duly developed, and production of the "Bertha" was duly transferred there. The company's design offices remained at Augsburg.

In June 1937, the Bf 109 V10 flew for the first time with the promising 960hp Daimler-Benz DB 600Aa fitted. This new powerplant was much longer and heavier than the Jumo, and in order to offset the shift in the aircraft's center of gravity, Messerschmitt redesigned the fighter's cooling system. A shallow radiator bath was fitted under the nose and two radiators positioned beneath the wings. A three-bladed VDM propeller also replaced the two-blade VDM-Hamilton airscrew fitted to the Jumo-powered Bf 109B. Due to the fighter's increased all up weight, its fuselage and undercarriage were also strengthened. This aircraft would effectively serve as the prototype for the Bf 109E.

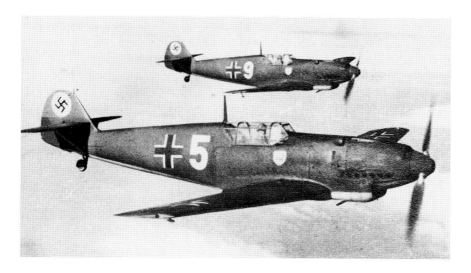

Among the first Bf 109B-2s to enter frontline service in the spring of 1937 were these aircraft of I./JG 132, based at Jüterbog-Damm. This unit would subsequently become Jagdgeschwader 2 "Richthofen" in May 1939.

In the early spring of 1938 deliveries of the Bf 109C, fitted with the 730hp fuel-injected Jumo 210Ga engine and wing-mounted machine guns, commenced, with the first aircraft being issued to I./JG 132. Only 58 were built prior to production switching to the four-gun Bf 109D, which was powered by the 680hp carburetored Jumo 210Da engine. Some 657 were built, with aircraft also being constructed by Erla Maschinenwerk in Leipzig and Focke-Wulf Flugzeugbau of Bremen.

By September 19, 1938, the Luftwaffe had 583 Bf 109B/C/Ds on strength, but limited availability of the Daimler-Benz engine stymied plans for the rapid fielding of the Bf 109E. This was because bomber production had priority over fighter procurement in the late 1930s, and most DB 600 production was allocated to the He 111.

Finally, in 1938, the focus shifted to fighter production, and by then the much-delayed DB 601A was at last reaching maturity, so Daimler-Benz switched its efforts to perfecting this powerplant. This new engine was very similar to the DB 600, but crucially it featured fuel injection rather than a float carburetor. This meant that the Bf 109 could perform negative G flight, and also increased the fighter's range through improved fuel economy.

With its DB 601A engine rated at 1,175hp for take-off, the Bf 109E-1 finally entered series production in December 1938, the new aircraft boasting unmatched take-off and climb performance. The higher wing loading of the "Emil" increased the fighter's turning circle and stall speed, but it was still very much a pilot's aircraft.

Like the D-model before it, the E-1's armament consisted of two 7.92mm MG 17s in the upper fuselage decking and two more machine guns in the wings. The latter had 500 rounds per gun, and the fuselage guns had 1,000 rounds each.

In early 1939 the first Bf 109E-3s began rolling off the production line, these aircraft having their wing MG 17s replaced with MG FF 20mm cannon as initially trialed in the Bf 109C-3. Each weapon only had 60 rounds, but their destructive punch was unrivaled. Once in frontline service, the E-3 "Kanonenmaschine" was rated as the best early generation Messerschmitt by those that flew it, with the aircraft enjoying a greater margin of superiority over its rivals than any other Bf 109 variant.

Between January 1 and September 1, 1939, 1,091 "Emils" were delivered. Four engine plants had been established to allow production of the DB 601 to keep apace with airframe construction, with Bf 109s being built by Messerschmitt, Erla and Fieseler in Germany, and by the Wiener-Neüstadt Flugzeugbau in Austria.

By the time the Wehrmacht advanced east into Poland on September 1, 1939, no fewer than 28 Gruppen were operating Bf 109B/C/D/Es. The Messerschmitt fighter was now well placed to dominate the skies over Europe.

In the autumn of 1940, Messerschmitt's E-model replacement in the form of the Bf 109F-1 began rolling off production lines in Germany. This aircraft differed from its predecessor primarily in its weaponry. The F-model saw the wing guns deleted in favor of a single engine-mounted cannon firing through the propeller hub, in addition to two upper cowling-mounted machine guns. Various hydraulic and cooling system improvements were also incorporated, as was additional pilot and fuel tank armor. Externally, the fighter was also more streamlined around the nose, and lengthened overall. The tail section was tidied up aerodynamically, with the deletion of the horizontal stabilizer bracing. Finally, the F-model's wing was completely redesigned, with the wingtips extended and rounded.

Production of the Bf 109F numbered 3,300+ airframes built over four sub-variants (F-1 to F-4), and ran from September 1940 through to May 1942. Like the "Emil," the "Friedrich" performed both fighter and fighter-bomber missions in eastern and western Europe, the Mediterranean and in North Africa.

The F-model was replaced on the production line in June 1942 by the Bf 109G, which combined the "Friedrich's" refined airframe with the larger, heavier and considerably more powerful 1,475hp DB 605 engine. Cockpit pressurization was also introduced for the first time with the G-1, although most later sub-variants lacked this feature. Produced in staggering numbers from mid-1942 through to war's end, some 24,000+ Bf 109Gs were constructed in total – including an overwhelming 14,212 in 1944 alone.

A III./JG 2 Gruppe *Spiess* (senior NCO), with his hand on the exhaust shroud, supervises the return of a Bf 109F-2 into its small wooden hangar at St Pol in the summer of 1941.

Numerous modifications to the basic G-1 were introduced either in the factory (as *Umrüst-Bausätze* factory conversion sets) or in the field (*Rüstsätze*), and these included the provision for extra armament, additional radios, introduction of a wooden tailplane, the fitting of a lengthened tailwheel and the installation of the MW-50 water/methanol-boosted DB 605D engine. In an attempt to standardize the equipment of the frontline force, Messerschmitt began production of the Bf 109G-6 in February 1943, and this model included many of these previously ad hoc additions. The G-6 would ultimately prove to be the most important variant of Messerschmitt's famous fighter, with 12,000+ examples being built – more than a third of the overall production run for the Bf 109.

Unfortunately, the continual addition of weighty items like underwing cannon gondolas, rocket tubes and larger engines to the once slight airframe of the Bf 109 eliminated much of the fighter's once legendary maneuverability, and instead served to emphasize the aircraft's poor slow-speed performance, tricky lateral control and ground handling.

Yet in the late-war Bf 109G-10 model, fitted with the Erla Haube bulged canopy, tall wooden tailplane and DB 605D engine, Messerschmitt had a fighter capable of achieving speeds up to 429mph at 24,280ft. Confusingly, although the G-10 appeared numerically after the lightened G-14 in the sub-variant list for the Bf 109G, it was in fact the last production G-model to see service!

The last main operational version of the Bf 109 was the K-series, which was developed directly from the "Gustav." The K-4 was the only sub-variant to see frontline service, and this aircraft boasted a DB 605DM engine, wooden tail construction and single cannon and twin machine gun armament.

All major Bf 109G/K variants that fought with the P-47 in 1943–45 are described in detail in the next chapter.

Bf 109G-6s of III./JG 3 are refueled at Leipheim between missions flown in defense of Berlin in early March 1944. These Jagdwaffe fighters had just clashed with P-47s and P-51s in a series of ferocious battles over the German capital, the USAAF fighters attempting to protect Eighth Air Force B-17s that had been sent to bomb Berlin in daylight for the very first time.

TECHNICAL SPECIFICATIONS

P-47 THUNDERBOLT

P-47B

Initial production version which differed from the prototype only in having a sliding hood in place of the hinged canopy, an SCR-774 radio (with a redesigned forward-slanted aerial), metal-skinned control surfaces, production 2,000hp R-2800-21 engine and General Electric A-13 turbosupercharger. The addition of internal operational equipment increased the aircraft's gross weight by 1,270lb to 13,356lb, although maximum level speed was increased to 429mph. The first five B-models built became pre-production test and evaluation aircraft. A total of 171 P-47Bs completed in total, all at Farmingdale.

P-47C

Similar to the P-47B, the P-47C-1-RE (RE was factory designation for Farmingdale) was fitted with a 2,300hp R-2800-59 that featured an A-17 turbosupercharger regulator. Aircraft also had a slightly longer forward fuselage, which had been extended 8in. at the firewall (increasing overall length from 35ft to 36ft 1in.) to create a better center of gravity and make the engine accessories compartment roomier and easier to work in. This variant also had the provision for a belly-mounted bomb or drop tank. The C-2-RE featured a metal-covered rudder and elevators, as well as a revised oxygen

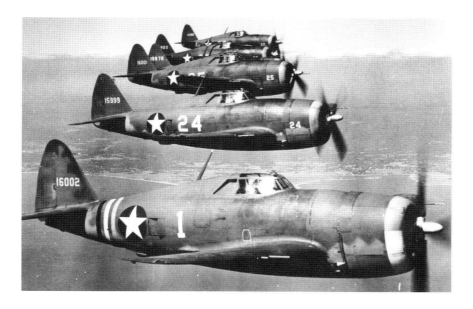

system. The follow-on C-5-RE had an upright radio mast in place of the forward-sloped example previously fitted. The first P-47C was completed on September 14, 1942, and a total of 602 were eventually built.

P-47D-1 THROUGH TO D-10

The D-1-RA (114 built) was the first P-47 model to emerge from the new Evansville, Indiana, plant from December 1942 – RA was the Evansville factory designation. It was essentially similar to the C-5. The D-1-RE had additional cowling flaps, improved pilot armor and a new radio mast – all 105 were built at Farmingdale. The D-2-RA (200 built) was similar to the D-1-RE, as was the D-2-RE (445 built), which also featured minor upgrades to the fuel system. Some 100 D-3-RAs were then constructed, and these were similar to the D-2-RE. The D-5-RE (300 built) was based on the D-1-RE, but with modifications to the aircraft's fuel and hydraulic systems. The D-4-RA (200 built) was similar to the D-5-RE. The D-6-RE (350 built) was effectively a D-1-RE with two-point shackles for a bomb or a drop tank under the fuselage. The D-10-RE (250 built) was also based on the D-1-RE, but with further improvements to the hydraulic system and the fitment of a General Electric C-23 turbosupercharger.

P-47D-11 THROUGH TO D-23

The D-11-RE (400 built) was fitted with a 2,300hp R-2800-63 engine that featured water injection, as was the identical Evansville D-11-RA (250 built). The D-15-RE (496 built) introduced single stations for a bomb or drop tank beneath each wing panel and an increased payload that meant it could carry two 1,000lb or three 500lb bombs. The D-15-RA (157 built) was identical in specification. The D-16-RE (254 built) was based on the D-11-RE, but it could run on 100/150 octane fuel – just 29 D-16-RAs

The distinctively marked engine cowling panels of a 84th FS/78th FG P-47D-22 "razorback" are carefully positioned in front of the fighter at Duxford in the early spring of 1944. This aircraft was one of the first natural metal Thunderbolts to arrive in the ETO from America. It was assigned to Capt Quince Brown, who claimed 12.333 aerial kills, including seven Bf 109s, prior to being shot down by flak on September 6, 1944 and executed by an SS officer.

of a similar specification were built. The D-20-RE (250 built) was powered by a 2,300hp R-2800-59, and it also had a raised tailwheel strut, General Electric ignition harness and other minor airframe modifications – Evansville built 187 D-20-RAs to an identical specification. Delivered in natural metal finish, the D-21-RE (216 built) had manual water injection control for the engine, but was otherwise similar to the D-11-RE. The D-21-RA (224 built) was essentially the same as the D-21-RE. The D-22-RE (850 built) featured the 13ft Hamilton Standard paddle-blade propeller and an A-23 turbosupercharger regulator. Featuring the same engine modification, the D-23-RA (889 built) was fitted with a Curtiss Electric 13ft paddle-blade propeller.

P-47D-25 WING GUNS

All versions of the P-47 Thunderbolt were armed with either six or eight Browning M-2 0.50-in. machine guns, split three or four per wing. The wing magazines contained 425 rounds per gun, although this number had to be reduced to 267 rounds per gun from the P-47D-15 onwards if the fighter was carrying a bombload of 1,000lb or additional fuel tanks affixed to its newly introduced underwing pylons (one per wing).

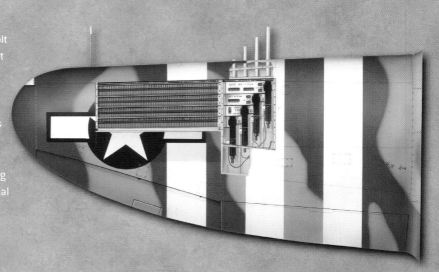

P-47D-25 THROUGH TO D-40

The D-25-RE (385 built) was the first P-47 fitted with a teardrop canopy and cut-down rear fuselage. The aircraft also had an increased supply of oxygen and some of its fuselage-located systems repositioned to allow its fuel capacity to be increased to 270 US gallons. The D-26-RA (250 built) was similar to the D-25-RE, as was the D-27-RE (615 built) bar minor fuel system modifications. The D-28-RA (1,028 built) was based on the D-26-RA. The D-28-RE (750 built) was similar to the D-25-RE, although it was fitted with a Curtiss Electric 13ft paddle-blade propeller. The D-30-RE (800 built) was also based on the D-25-RE, but it had five stubs beneath each wing for High-Velocity Aerial Rockets – the D-30-RA (1,800 built) was built to the same specification. The final D-model sub-variants to be built were the D-35-RA and D-40-RA, of which 665 were constructed in 1944–45. These versions featured a dorsal fin for increased stability.

P-47G

Basically similar to the C-1-RE, 20 P-47G-CUs were the first Thunderbolts built on the new Curtiss-Wright line at Buffalo, New York, in late 1942. These were fitted with R-2800-21 engines and Curtiss Electric 12ft 2in. propellers. Subsequent production covered the G-1-CU (40 built), similar to the C-5-RE, G-5-CU (60 built), similar to the D-1-RE, G-10-CU (80 built), similar to the D-6-RE, and G-15-CU (154 built), similar to the D-11-RE. Most were assigned to training units in the USA, where they were fitted with the mounting points for a blind-flying hood inside the canopy. They were designated as TP-47Gs when used by training units.

P-47D-28 44-19790 has its R2800 fettled in the autumn sunshine outside the No. 2 hangar at Boxted on October 11, 1944. This aircraft was assigned to Capt Michael Jackson of the 56th FG's 62nd FS, the eight-kill ace scoring five of his victories (including two Bf 109s) in 44-19790.

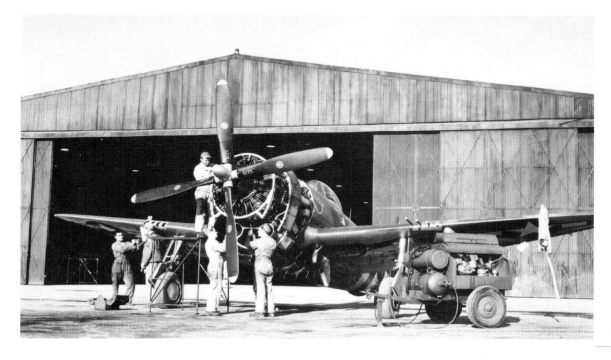

P-47M-1

Farmingdale hastily constructed the M-1-RE (130 built), featuring a 2,800hp R-2800-57 with an uprated CH-5 turbosupercharger. The aircraft was also fitted with airbrakes in the wings, but was otherwise identical to the D-30-RE. All were sent to the 56th FG in the autumn of 1944, where dorsal fins were fitted in the field.

P-47N

The final production variant, the N-1-RE (550 built) saw the P-47D-27-RE fuselage, fitted with an R-2800-57 engine and CH-5 turbosupercharger driving a Curtiss Electric 13ft paddle-blade propeller, combined with a new long-span wing 18in. greater in span and 22 sq. ft larger in area. The latter also incorporated larger ailerons and square-cut tips. Numerous detail design changes were also incorporated, and extra fuel in the wings gave a total of 186 US gallons – single 300 US gallon drop tanks could be carried beneath each wing. A further 550 N-5-REs followed, and these were similar to the N-1-REs bar the addition of rocket launchers, AN/APS-13 tail warning radar and provision for a General Electric C-1 autopilot. N-15-RE (200 built) similar to N-1-RE except for the addition of an S-1 bomb rack and K-14A/B gunsight. N-20-RE (200 built) similar to N-1-RE, bar a new radio, as was the N-20-RA (149 built) except for minor cockpit changes. N-25-RE (167 built) was the final production version, and this too was similar to the N-1-RE except for the addition of autopilot, a new cockpit floor and strengthened ailerons to deflect rocket blast.

Bf 109G/K

Bf 109G-1 AND -2

Although looking very similar to the Bf 109F, the G-series was built to take advantage of the increased power output of the DB 605 engine, and the ability of the latter to be power-boosted to increase its performance in speed and altitude. Pressurized versions were also built in an effort to counter increased high altitude raids being made by USAAF heavy bombers. Additional armor was also a feature of G-series aircraft, as was their improved armament, whereby rifle-caliber machine guns were replaced by hard-hitting 13mm, 20mm and 30mm cannon. This also meant the return of wing armament. Both the G-1 and -2 entered service in June 1942, with the former being pressurized for high altitude combat and latter unpressurized. Both were to be powered by the DB 605A, B or C, with each version being essentially the same bar different gear ratios – early G-1s also featured GM 1 nitrous oxide power boosting. Armament initially consisted of two nose-mounted MG 17 7.9mm machine guns and a hub-firing MG 151 20mm cannon. A G-2 Trop version was used in tropical and rough theaters such as North Africa, this variant having additional engine filtering.

This Bf 109G-1 was assigned to P-47 killer Leutnant Heinz Knoke of II./JG 11 in the summer of 1943. The aircraft boasts underwing rocket tubes. Keen eyes will also note the absence of the additional air scoop above the supercharger air intake which normally characterized the high-altitude G-1 (this was presumably due to a replacement cowling being fitted from a non-pressurized "Gustav").

Like all G-series aircraft, many G-1/2s were modified in the field to meet specific operational requirements. These Rüstsätze alterations allowed the aircraft to be carry a centerline bomb rack (R1 and R2), drop tank (R3) or anti-personnel bombs (R4), underwing MG 151 pods (R6), or fuselage-mounted cameras (R2, and R3 from 1943). Some 164 G-1s and 1,614 G-2s were built.

Bf 109G-3 AND -4

The unpressurized Bf 109G-4 actually appeared in the front line before the pressurized G-3, making its combat debut in November 1942. A total of 1,100 G-4s were produced between September 1942 and May 1943 (with additional aircraft built in Hungary between July and September 1943). Just 50 G-3s were constructed in January–February 1943. The G-3/4 differed from the G-1/2 by having a FuG 16Z radio installed in place of the FuG 7a – the aerial wire arrangement was changed also. The Rüstsätze sets made available were identical in content and designation to those fitted to the G-1/2, and Messerschmitt also produced an Umrüst-Bauzätze U modification for the G-3 too. Designated the U2, it referred to an uprated type of GM 1 power-boosting, combined with the fitment of a propeller from an Me 210.

Bf 109G-5 AND -6

The unpressurized Bf 109G-6 and pressurized G-5 were issued to frontline units from February and September 1943, respectively. In their initial form, they only differed from the G-3/4 in having cowling-mounted MG 131 13mm machine guns rather than MG 17 7.9mm weapons. The large breech blocks associated with the MG 131 could only be housed by modifying the upper fuselage engine cowlings to incorporate distinctive beulen (boils) that in turn came to symbolize all late war Bf 109Gs.

Powered by a DB 605A with GM 1 or a DB 605AS incorporating the larger supercharger of the DB 603 (designated the G-5/AS, and with no beulen), less than 500 G-5s were built. These were the last pressurized Bf 109s constructed for frontline use, as cockpit pressurization was found to be of dubious operational value. Once again, with the G-5 the Rüstsätze sets made available were identical in content and designation to those fitted to previous G-series aircraft, with the addition of the R2 (reconnaissance), R5 (underwing cannon pods) and R7 (extra navigation aids). Umrüst-Bauzätze U modifications, often combined with Rüstsätze sets, were also produced, with the U2 being GM 1 power-boosted and featuring a wooden tailplane of increased height (and revised fin-and-rudder assembly), and the U4 having a MK 108 30mm cannon replacing the hub-firing MG 151. Finally, the Bf 109G-5/AS was powered by the DB 605AS engine, and its supercharger was housed within a bulged fairing on the port side of the forward fuselage – this variant had no beulen as a result. Unlike the G-5, the Bf 109G-6 was built in staggering numbers, with more than 12,000 examples rolling off production lines between the late autumn of 1942 and June 1944. Built as the first "standard" model "Gustav" that was intended from the outset to accept any of the ever-increasing number of Rüstsätze sets emanating from Messerschmitt, the G-6 was also capable of being powered by several versions of the DB 605A – the uprated DB 605D was also made available from January 1944. The G-6 was also the first "Gustav" variant capable of carrying the engine-mounted MK 108 cannon. However, production of this awesome 30mm weapon was delayed to the extent that a considerable number of G-6s were built with the MG 151 fitted instead. As with the G-5, the Rüstsätze sets available for the G-6 followed the R designation pattern put in place with the G-1/2. The only real changes unique to

Bf 109G-5/6 UPPER COWLING GUNS

Like previous versions of the Bf 109, the "Gustav" was fitted with a pair of upper cowling guns. These had initially taken the form of Rheinmetall MG 17 7.92mm weapons, but from the G-5/6 onwards, the weapons installed were MG 131 13mm machine guns produced by the same company. Each weapon had a magazine holding 300 rounds.

this variant centered on the late (1944) R2 set, which covered the fitment of a single WGr 21 mortar launcher beneath each wing. Numerous Umrüst-Bauzätze modifications were to feature, however, starting with the U2 that saw the fighter fitted with a GM 1-boosted engine and a wooden tailplane similar to that used by the G-5/U2. The U4 saw the MK 108 replace the MG 151, while the U5 had underwing MK 108s instead of the 20mm cannon. The U6 was similarly armed, but also had the engine-mounted MG 151 replaced with a MK 108 too. Various G-6s had clear vision Erla Haube hoods fitted in the field in place of the conventional framed canopy. Finally, the Bf 109G-6/AS was powered by the DB 605AS engine, and like the G-5/AS, it had a supercharger bulge rather than MG 131 beulen.

Bf 109G-8

Produced in small numbers, the G-8 was a specialized tactical photo-reconnaissance version of the G-6 that was built to support ground forces. This variant appeared in August 1943, and featured a vertically-mounted camera (either an RB 12.5/7 or RB 32/7) in the center fuselage. Again, the Rüstsätze sets available for the G-8 followed the R designation pattern put in place with the G-1/2, with the only unique one to this variant being the R5 set which saw the aircraft fitted with a FuG 16 ZS radio – the latter operated on Army frequencies. Two Umrüst-Bauzätze kits were also made available, with the U2 seeing the aircraft fitted with the GM 1-boosted engine modification and the U3 featuring a DB 605D with MW 50 methanol-water injection. All G-8s had their MG 131 fuselage guns deleted, the aircraft relying on the hub-firing MK 108 or MG 151 for self-defense.

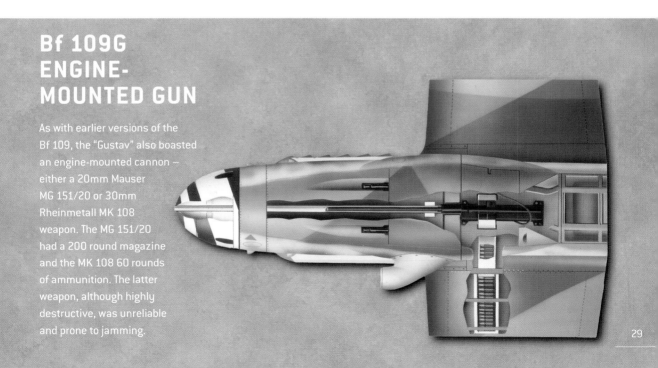

Bf 109G ENGINE-MOUNTED GUN

As with earlier versions of the Bf 109, the "Gustav" also boasted an engine-mounted cannon — either a 20mm Mauser MG 151/20 or 30mm Rheinmetall MK 108 weapon. The MG 151/20 had a 200 round magazine and the MK 108 60 rounds of ammunition. The latter weapon, although highly destructive, was unreliable and prone to jamming.

A Bf 109G-6/R6 of I./JG 27 is seen on patrol near Frankfurt on May 12, 1944. It bears "black double chevron" Gruppenkommandeur markings on the fuselage, as well as sage green Defense of the Reich bands aft of the gray and white, vice black and white, Balkenkruez. Note the fighter's underwing MG 151/20 cannon pods.

Bf 109G-12

Produced ahead of the Bf 109G-14 and G-10, the G-12 was a dedicated two-seat trainer version of the "Gustav" created through the conversion of existing G-2/4/6 airframes. A total of 494 G-12s were modified by Blohm & Voss between September 1943 and December 1944. To make room for the second seat, the aircraft's fuel capacity was reduced from 400 to 235 liters. The instructor sat in the rear seat and spoke with the student pilot via an intercom. The sole Rüstsätze kit available for the G-12 was the R3, which allowed the aircraft to carry a 300-liter drop tank.

Bf 109G-14

Very similar in specification and appearance to late-build G-6s, the DB 605AM-powered Bf 109G-14 began appearing in the front line in July 1944 after Messerschmitt decided to incorporate the MW 50 power-boost as standard equipment on all piston-engined fighters then in production – this was previously available as the U3 modification on the G-6. The G-14 also had the FuG 16ZY radio fitted as standard too, this equipment being retrofitted to late-build G-6s. The Rüstsätze kits available for the aircraft covered fighter-bomber conversion with a bomb rack (R1), extended range with a 300-liter drop tank (R3), heavy fighter with two underwing MG 151s (R5) and an all-weather fighter with autopilot and FuG 125 radio (R6). The sole Umrüst-Bauzätze kit was the U4, which saw the G-14 replace its hub-firing MG 151 with a MK 108, and a wooden tail assembly fitted instead of one in metal. The Bf 109G-14/AS was powered by the DB 605AS engine, and like the G-5/AS, it had a supercharger bulge rather than MG 131 beulen. The Erla Haube hood was widely fitted to this variant, but it did not totally replace the original framed G-model canopy. The aircraft had an underwing Morane mast as well as a Zielfluganlage D/F loop and a FuG 25a IFF antenna below the fuselage.

Bf 109G-10

Appearing after the Bf 109K series, and thus earning the distinction of being the last sub-type built before war's end, the Bf 109G-10 first appeared in the autumn of 1944. Officially defined as a "bastard type" by the Luftwaffe, the aircraft combined the 1,850hp methanol-water injected DB 605DM engine of the Bf 109K-4 with the G-14/AS airframe. However, a chronic shortage of these engines saw DB 605ASs routinely fitted in their place, and as with all AS-powered Bf 109G/Ks, these particular aircraft had a supercharger bulge rather than MG 131 beulen. As with the G-12, the Erla Haube hood was widely fitted to this variant also, but once again it did not totally replace the original framed G-model canopy. The Rüstsätze kits available were identical to those for the G-14, with the addition of the R2 reconnaissance fit that included RB 50/30 or RB 75/30 cameras, the R7 underwing WGr 21 launcher kit and the R8, which featured a BSK 16 gun camera. And like the G-14, the only Umrüst-Bauzätze kit for the G-10 was the U4, which replaced the hub-firing MG 151 with a MK 108, and saw a wooden tail assembly fitted instead of a metal one.

Bf 109K-4

Continuing delays with the mass production of new German jet fighters forced the RLM to keep building Bf 109s until war's end. Realizing that production of various Umrüst-Bauzätze and Rüstsätze kits was slowing overall production, the RLM decided to rationalize things by ordering Messerschmitt to incorporate the best of the G-model upgrades into a single airframe, which was in turn designated the Bf 109K-4. Like the G-10 (which actually appeared after the K-4), the new aircraft

This posed photograph of 11./JG 3's "Yellow 1," taken in January 1945, illustrates all the salient features of the Bf 109K-4 – the "unbulged" cowling associated with the DB 605DM engine, mainwheel doors, repositioned dorsal fuel filler cap (indicated by the warning triangle), which was moved forward one frame and displaced the D/F loop to its rear, and long-legged retractable tailwheel.

would be powered by the DB 605DM with MW 50 boost. The K-model would also incorporate as much non-strategic material (such as wood and steel sheeting) within its structure as was possible. The armament was upgraded to two 13mm MG 131 machine guns in the cowling and a hub-firing MK 108 30mm cannon. As with several other late-build variants of the Bf 109G, the aircraft's tail assembly was made entirely of wood, and a longer, retractable, tailwheel was also fitted to some, but not all, K-4s. Yet another late-build G-model modification to be found in the K-4 was the employment of broad chord propeller blades. The fighter also lacked an antenna mast. The first K-4s entered service in October 1944, and they were the only sub-type of the final Bf 109 series to see combat – some 1,500+ had been built by VE-Day. Again, Rüstsätze kits were available, covering the fitment of a bomb rack (R1), RB 50/30 or RB 75/30 cameras and FuG 16ZS radio (R2), extended range 300-liter drop tank (R3), two underwing MG 151s (R4) and the installation of a BSK 16 gun camera (R6) in the left wing. Many K-4s had no MG 131 beulen, and most were fitted with the Erla Haube hood. Finally, the aircraft had an underwing Morane mast as well as a Zielfluganlage D/F loop and a FuG 25a IFF antenna beneath the fuselage. There were no Umrüst-Bauzätze kits produced by Messerschmitt for the K-4.

Bf 109G UNDERWING GUN

The "Gustav" could supplement its engine and cowling guns with two 20mm Mauser MG 151/20 cannon in underwing gondolas (a MK 108-equipped gondola was also developed). These were fitted to the aircraft as part of a field-installed Rüstsätze R kit. Each weapon drew its ammunition from a 120-round magazine. The widely used G-6 was the version most associated with underwing cannon, with this fitment rarely being seen on subsequent "Gustav" variants.

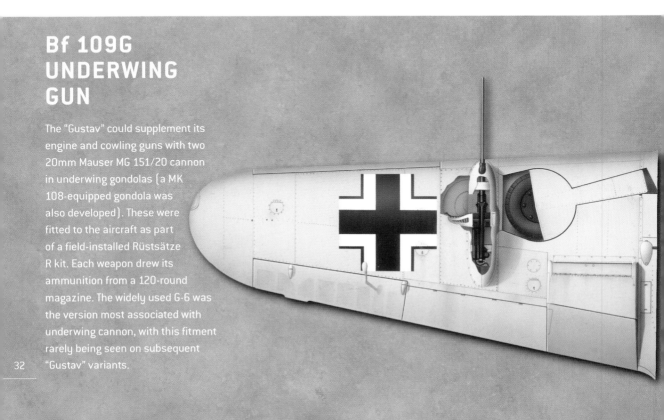

P-47D THUNDERBOLT and Bf 109G COMPARISON SPECIFICATIONS

	P-47D-25	Bf 109G-6
Powerplant	2,300hp R-2800-59	1,800hp DB 605AM
Dimensions		
Span	40ft 9.25in.	32ft 6.5in.
Length	36ft 1.75in.	29ft 7in.
Height	14ft 2in.	8ft 2.5in.
Wing area	300 sq. ft	174.37 sq. ft
Weights		
Empty	10,000lb	5,893lb
Loaded	19,400lb	7,491lb
Performance		
Max speed	429mph at 27,800ft	385mph at 22,640ft
Range	475 miles (without tanks)	447 miles (without tanks)
Climb	to 20,000ft in 11 min.	to 18,700ft in 6 min.
Service ceiling	42,000ft	37,890ft
Armament:	8 x 0.50-in. Brownings	2 x 13mm MG 131 1 x 20mm MG 151

Firmly chocked, a Bf 109G-14 of 9./JG 26 has its DB 605AM engine run up at Lille-Nord just a few weeks prior to the D-Day landings. The distinctive beulen synonymous with late-build "Gustavs" are clearly visible in this close-up view. Note also the original-style canopy and 300-liter centerline drop tank.

THE STRATEGIC SITUATION

Following the invasion of the Soviet Union in June 1941, the Jagdwaffe fighter force in the west consisted of JG 1 in north-west Germany, JG 26 in the Pas de Calais and the Low Countries and JG 2 defending the Atlantic coast ports of France. JG 2 and JG 26 had nine Staffeln each (a Staffel having a strength of 12 aircraft), grouped into three Gruppen apiece. A total of around 200 Bf 109E/Fs therefore defended the Channel front at any given time in 1941–42.

At intervals, Gruppen or Staffeln from JG 2 and JG 26 would be sent to other fronts, and their place taken by units from *Jagdgeschwaderen* posted in from the Mediterranean or the Eastern Front. Such rotation allowed the Luftwaffe to maintain its fighter strength at approximately 200 aircraft.

With Allied air power in the West steadily increasing throughout 1942, and the USAAF's Eighth Air Force arriving in the UK in the late summer of that year, this force of 200 Bf 109Fs and Fw 190As found it increasingly hard to repel daylight bombing raids on industrial and strategic targets. In the spring of 1943, when the P-47 groups of VIII Fighter Command commenced operations in defense of USAAF heavy bombers, the Jagdwaffe in the west was forced to call on reinforcements from Gruppen in the east. By late July, a further five Jagdgruppen had been withdrawn from the southern USSR and Italy and sent to Germany to strengthen the day fighter arm defending the Third Reich.

One of the first units pulled back was Bf 109G-equipped III./JG 54, which arrived from the east in February 1943. I./JG 27 followed from North Africa shortly afterwards, and the last of the trio of "Gustav"-equipped Gruppen posted in was I./JG 3, transferred west from Stalingrad.

A further increase in the ranks of the Jagdwaffe in the west was achieved in April when two of JG 1's four Gruppen were redesignated as units of the newly-formed JG 11, which continued to fly Bf 109Gs. Thus, by mid-1943, the Bf 109 strength in the west consisted of eight main Gruppen, five of which were deployed along the Channel and North Sea coastlines from the Biscay to the German Bight – the main routes used by the Eighth Air Force.

From west to east, the five Gruppen were II./JG 2, III./JG 26, III./JG 54 and II. and III./JG 11. The first two units formed part of Luftflotte 3, which was the frontline "air fleet" guarding outermost ramparts of occupied north-western Europe. Bf 109G-equipped I./JG 27 was also part of Luftflotte 3, as was III./JG 54 for a short while. The three Bf 109 Gruppen of JGs 1 and 11, together with I./JG 3, were subordinated to Luftwaffenbefehlshaber Mitte (the forerunner of Luftflotte Reich) purely for defense of the homeland, however. Sitting astride the "heavies'" main routes of approach into north-western Germany, JGs 1 and 11 bore the brunt of much of the action in 1943.

The early official pedantry issued by Luftwaffe HQ that the Bf 109 units were to engage only fighter escorts that were in attendance, leaving the Fw 190As to concentrate on the bomber boxes, soon became an irrelevance in the heat of battle. Now, entire Gruppen and, on occasion, Geschwader of defending fighters would be sent up to do battle in the latter half of 1943 where previously single *Schwärme* or Staffeln had sufficed.

Buoyed by its successes against the USAAF heavy bombers in the summer, the Jagdwaffe introduced a second wave of reinforcements to the Reich's Defense organization in the autumn of 1943. II. and III./JG 3 were duly pulled out of Russia and sent to join I./JG 3 in western Germany. In line with persisting doctrine, which stipulated that home defense Geschwader should consist of two anti-bomber Gruppen and one Gruppe of covering fighters, II./JG 3 received a batch of new Bf 109G-5 high altitude fighters to add to its G-6s. In reality, the "light" fighter Gruppe would down as many bombers as fighters in coming months.

II./JG 27 and II./JG 51 were also transferred in for Homeland defense from Italy at this time, both units again being equipped with Bf 109Gs. These new Gruppen

These new Bf 109G-6/R6 "gunboats" from I./JG 27 were photographed at Fels am Wagram, in Austria, in early 1944. Both aircraft have freshly applied Defense of the Reich bands just forward of their tailplanes. These markings were introduced in January 1944. Note also 3. Staffel's "Staffel Marseille" emblem on the nose of the "Gustav" closest to the camera.

combined with those already in-theater to inflict such severe losses on USAAF bomber formations during raids on Schweinfurt and Regensburg in August, September and October that the Americans halted long-range penetration missions until suitable fighter cover could be provided.

The Bf 109G was in the vanguard of these missions, and the defense of Germany in the late summer and early autumn of 1943 marked the pinnacle of the Jagdwaffe's performance in the west. From then on, as the Eighth Air Force's fortunes improved with the fielding of genuine escort fighters in the form of drop tank-equipped Thunderbolts and the arrival of the superb Merlin-engined Mustang, the German fighter force would find itself in an ever-steepening spiral of decline.

Despite the bloody reversals over Schweinfurt and Regensburg, USAAF senior planners were generally of the opinion that precision bombing attacks by B-17 Flying Fortresses and B-24 Liberators could be flown in daylight against targets in Europe without escort and without suffering heavy losses. Nothing the RAF or anyone else said was going to sway this dogmatic resolve, and some Eighth Air Force generals even believed that escort fighters were unnecessary. However, just as the Luftwaffe had discovered in 1940 during the Battle of Britain, VIII Bomber Command eventually realized that bomber losses could be reduced in proportion to the distance escorting fighters could escort the "heavies."

The Luftwaffe had been powerless to implement an effective strategy because a lack of organization in the production of fighters restricted the numbers of Bf 109s available to it in the summer and autumn of 1940. Those that did operate over Britain were severely restricted in radius of action by limited fuel reserves. The Luftwaffe was eventually forced to switch to night bombing, as was RAF Bomber Command when

Although senior personnel in the Luftwaffe wanted the more heavily armed Fw 190 to be the bomber killer, leaving the higher flying Bf 109 to deal with the escorting fighters, this photograph shows that "Gustav" pilots also received training in how best to down a "heavy." The experienced Jagdflieger appears to be advocating the head-on attack as the most effective way to engage a B-24 — the wire protruding from the latter illustrates the bomber's areas of defensive fire. Judging from their expressions, his audience — especially the pilot to his immediate right — seems to be far from convinced!

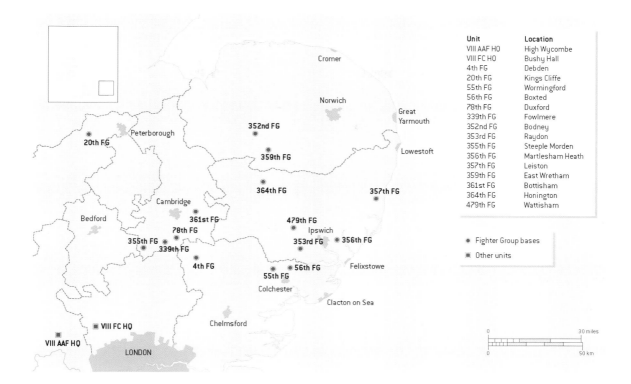

Unit	Location
VIII AAF HQ	High Wycombe
VIII FC HQ	Bushy Hall
4th FG	Debden
20th FG	Kings Cliffe
55th FG	Wormingford
56th FG	Boxted
78th FG	Duxford
339th FG	Fowlmere
352nd FG	Bodney
353rd FG	Raydon
355th FG	Steeple Morden
356th FG	Martlesham Heath
357th FG	Leiston
359th FG	East Wretham
361st FG	Bottisham
364th FG	Honington
479th FG	Wattisham

● Fighter Group bases
■ Other units

0   30 miles
0   50 km

horrendous daylight losses left it with little choice but to undertake nocturnal raids on German targets in 1941.

But even when American bomber losses reached epidemic proportions in the autumn of 1943, the Eighth Air Force never abandoned its daylight precision bombing concept. That the USAAF daylight offensive did not go the same way as that of the Luftwaffe and RAF Bomber Command is due entirely to the advent of the long-range escort fighter.

In the autumn of 1942, all but one of VIII Fighter Command's fighter groups (the 4th FG) had been transferred to North Africa in support of the Operation *Torch* landings. The rebuilding of the Eighth Air Force's fighter arm commenced in December of that year when the P-38-equipped 78th FG arrived in England from the US. A decision was then made to re-equip both groups with P-47C/D Thunderbolts, and VIII Fighter Command also welcomed the 56th FG in January 1943 – both the 4th and 78th re-equipped with Thunderbolts later that same month. All three units were declared operational with the P-47C in April, and by year-end there were ten Thunderbolt groups in England.

The Eighth Air Force planned on using the P-47 force to support its daylight bomber operations, but pilots new to the theater were first to gain operational experience under the watchful eye of RAF Fighter Command. Spitfires had been employed in offensive cross-Channel operations since early 1941, mostly on *Rodeos*, whereby several squadrons carried out a high-speed sweep over France or the Low Countries to lure Bf 109s into combat. However, the Luftwaffe often refused to take

VIII Fighter Command's fighter groups were based in East Anglia so that they could be as close to targets in Occupied Europe as possible. Most of these airfields were built from scratch specially for the USAAF in a massive construction program launched in 1942.

the bait, so a *Circus* consisting of a small number of bombers with strong fighter support was despatched. A fighter escort for a dedicated bomber operation was known as a *Ramrod*.

When planning P-47 operations, the prime consideration in 1943 was range. Early Thunderbolt missions without belly tanks lasted between 1hr 45min and 2hrs 5min. With 75-gal pressurized tanks, missions could last up to 2hrs 50min. The 165-gal tanks gave another 45–50 minutes' range, and with aircraft utilizing two 108-gal wing tanks, P-47 groups could fly sorties that lasted up to 5hrs 30min – made of metal, the 108-gal tanks were initially in very short supply. The far more common treated pressed-paper wing tanks gave further range, but they also caused some problems.

The paper tanks were sometimes difficult to drop in combat because they occasionally froze at high altitude. One of the tricks used to jettison a recalcitrant tank was to have a wingman slip his wingtip between the tank and the wing and knock it off the pylon! By late 1943, P-47 groups were using up to 480 tanks a month, and they tried to keep a six- to eight-mission back stock on hand. Fighter units were assigned their escort relay points by the size of the tanks they carried on the mission, which of course dictated their range.

Although the drop tanks gave the escort fighters a much-needed boost in their range, they had a detrimental impact on the handling of the Thunderbolt, as Col "Hub" Zemke recalled:

Flying a P-47 with a loaded tank was not a pleasant experience because the tank affected the aircraft's aerodynamics. I figured out that if the Luftwaffe caught us while hugging these things, we would be in trouble. Extra range, however, was a priority for our fighters due to the growing losses our B-17s were sustaining.

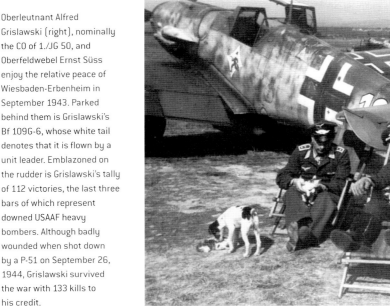

Oberleutnant Alfred Grislawski (right), nominally the CO of 1./JG 50, and Oberfeldwebel Ernst Süss enjoy the relative peace of Wiesbaden-Erbenheim in September 1943. Parked behind them is Grislawski's Bf 109G-6, whose white tail denotes that it is flown by a unit leader. Emblazoned on the rudder is Grislawski's tally of 112 victories, the last three bars of which represent downed USAAF heavy bombers. Although badly wounded when shot down by a P-51 on September 26, 1944, Grislawski survived the war with 133 kills to his credit.

In late 1943, when returning home from escort missions, Thunderbolt pilots began strafing targets of opportunity on the ground. The aircraft proved so successful in this role that the P-47D was subsequently adapted to carry wing-mounted bombs to add to the destructive power of its six or eight machine guns.

With more USAAF fighters now appearing over Germany, the Jagdwaffe quickly transferred in additional Bf 109G-equipped units in the shape of IV./JG 3 and II./JG 53 from Italy. Despite their arrival, and the bolstering of other Reich Defense units in Germany, the early months of 1944 were to prove costly for the Bf 109G Gruppen, as the rate of attrition amongst its experienced and irreplaceable leaders rose dramatically due to the extended range of the USAAF fighters. The latter were now spending much longer with the bombers, and their numbers were increasing all the time.

Four more Bf 109G-equipped Gruppen were added to the Homeland defensive line-up in the first half of 1944, as the Jagdwaffe struggled to make good rising losses. I./JG 5 arrived from Bulgaria in February, with II./JG 5 following two months later from the Arctic front. Finally, III. and IV./JG 27 moved north from Italy to Austria in March to protect southern Germany from strategic raids by the Fifteenth Air Force.

February–March 1944 proved to be the Thunderbolt's heyday when it came to air fighting with VIII Fighter Command. Thereafter, the Jagdwaffe would be more difficult to encounter, and the Mustang's advantage of greater endurance over the P-47 saw groups equipped with the North American fighter regularly running up substantial scores as they saw widespread use escorting long-penetration raids deep into Germany. The Mustang had the lowest fuel consumption rate of the three main USAAF fighters in the ETO, with the P-51B using 65 gal per hour compared with the P-47D, which consumed as much as 200 gal per hour, depending on power settings.

The P-51 equipped all but one of the Eighth Air Force's fighter groups by the late autumn of 1944, with most Thunderbolts in the ETO being used as fighter-bombers by units assigned to the tactical Ninth Air Force. These groups (some 13 in total) of IX and XIX Tactical Air Commands had departed bases in southern England for France shortly after the June 6, 1944 invasion of Normandy.

D-Day has seen Allied air forces boasting no fewer than 4,100 fighters, of which 2,300 were USAAF P-38s, P-47s and P-51s. In response, the Jagdwaffe could muster

Col "Hub" Zemke, CO of the 56th FG, was one of the great US fighter leaders of World War II. He is seen here admiring the wing guns of his P-47D for the benefit of the camera in early 1944.

just 425 Bf 109Gs and Fw 190As in Normandy, of which only 250–280 were serviceable on any given day.

In the lead up to D-Day, Channel-based JGs 2 and 26 had been bearing the full brunt of growing Allied air power. Unlike the Jagdgruppen stationed deep within Germany's borders, theirs was a campaign constantly being fought on two levels. For not only did they have to contend with high-flying US "heavies" attacking strategic targets within their own areas of responsibility (from U-boat pens in the west to airfields and industrial sites in the east) and beyond; they also had to oppose the swelling tide of tactical missions being mounted by the RAF and the Ninth Air Force as the coastal regions of north-west Europe were "softened up" ahead of the invasion.

Prior to the actual storming of the beaches of Normandy, despite lengthening casualty lists, the Jagdwaffe had managed to hold its own in the west. But in the wake of the invasion, the long retreat to final surrender had commenced.

The Luftwaffe had reacted quickly to the D-Day landings, and within hours of the first troops coming ashore, the whole Defense of the Reich organization that had been so painstakingly put together over past months was torn apart. By the evening of June 9, no fewer than 15 Jagdgruppen – all but four of then flying Bf 109Gs – had left Germany for the threatened Western Front. Although carefully assigned areas to

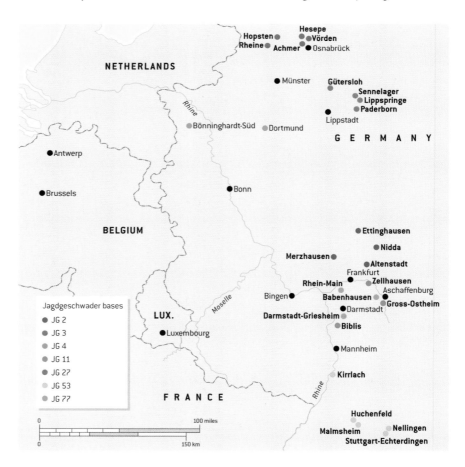

These were the principal Jagdwaffe Bf 109G/K bases at the time of Operation *Bodenplatte*, launched at dawn on January 1, 1945.

operate in, such was the Allies' overwhelming superiority (approaching 20-to-1 in fighter strength alone) that the Jagdgruppen soon abandoned their bases and began flying from widely dispersed, and heavily camouflaged, landing strips. Even here they were not safe from marauding fighter-bombers (including numerous P-47Ds from the Eighth and Ninth Air Forces), and by the end of June more than 350 German aircraft had been destroyed or damaged on the ground.

For many pilots who had only just begun to get to grips with the high-altitude anti-bomber air war over the Reich, the additional low-level dimension dictated by their opponents during the Normandy fighting proved too much. During the last three weeks of June more than 170 German fighter pilots were killed in action. Within a fortnight of their arrival in France, many Jagdgruppen had been reduced to single figure strength. Although the losses in men and machinery were constantly being made good, the inexperienced replacement pilots fared even worse. Nevertheless, the Bf 109G Gruppen still managed to claim a large number of Allied aircraft shot down, with the Ninth Air Force's P-47 fighter-bomber units suffering particularly badly.

And with more and more P-51s now being present in-theater, the Thunderbolts of the Eighth Air Force (now flown by just the 56th, 78th, 353rd and 356th FGs, as the remaining groups had switched to Mustangs) subsequently missed out on the renewed fighting over the German homeland in the late summer of 1944 primarily because the P-47 lacked the Mustang's endurance.

The aircraft being encountered by VIII Fighter Command in August were the surviving remnants of those Gruppen (together with JGs 2 and 26) that had been thrown into France three months earlier. They had now been ordered back to Germany, as the Jagdwaffe in the west was in irreversible decline. The units now fought alongside Gruppen that had been spared the carnage of Normandy, but had

This map reveals how the range of the P-47 was progressively extended through the introduction of ever larger external fuel tanks. Yet even when fitted with two underwing 108 gal tanks, the P-47D still only possessed half the endurance of a similarly equipped P-51D. Indeed, the latter could escort bombers to targets east of Vienna.

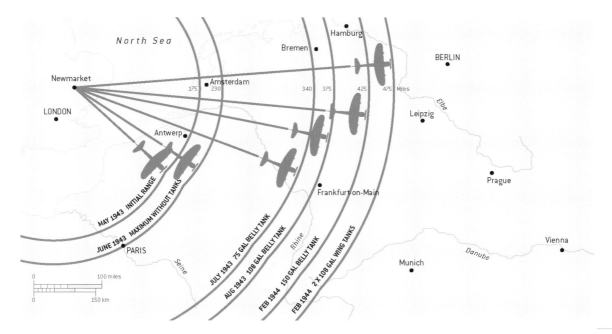

P-47D-16s of the Ninth Air Force's 378th FS/362nd FG await their next mission at a newly created airstrip in the Normandy region of France shortly after D-Day. The jerry cans in the foreground are being used to fill the refueling bowser to the left of the photograph – a laborious, and potentially dangerous, job. Once filled, the bowser would be towed out to the Thunderbolts and its contents rapidly pumped into the fighters' tanks. The majority of the groundcrewmen visible in this photograph are wearing their steel helmets, which indicates that the airfield was so close to the front line that they expected little warning should the Luftwaffe decide to mount a strafing attack on the strip.

nevertheless been fighting a war of attrition with Eighth Air Force "heavies," and their escorts. In July alone, Defense of the Reich units claimed 329 aircraft destroyed for the loss of 341 of their own. But whereas the former constituted just a fraction of the USAAF's strength (and could be rapidly replaced), the latter represented the equivalent of almost the entire Homeland single-seater defense force.

The return of the shattered remnants of the Normandy Gruppen brought no immediate relief to the embattled Defense of the Reich units either, for it would take several weeks before many of them could be deemed ready for frontline service again. Consequently, one final round of reinforcements was added to Homeland defense in the late summer and early autumn of 1944. Elements of JGs 4 and 77 were withdrawn from the southern and south-eastern perimeters of Hitler's rapidly shrinking "Fortress Europe," and two "new" Bf 109G Gruppen in I. and III./JG 76 – ex-*Zerstörer* units I./ZG 76 and II./ZG 1, respectively – were converted to "Gustavs." The latter soon became IV./JG 300 and IV./JG 53.

These new units, and the increased production of aircraft that saw no fewer than 3,013 single-seat fighters delivered to the Jagdwaffe in September 1944 alone, did little to improve the situation, however, as the Luftwaffe no longer had the infrastructure to support their effective employment, the fuel to power their aircraft or the trained pilots to fly them. Even the introduction of the Bf 109K-4 in October 1944 had virtually no impact on the aerial battles taking place over Germany, despite some 20 Jagdgruppen operating them alongside late-model "Gustavs" until war's end.

Both I. and II. Jagdkorps, which controlled fighter units in the west and in Defense of the Reich, continued to take the fight to the Allies as best they could. And in an effort to replicate the successes of Schweinfurt a year earlier, General der Jagdflieger Adolf Galland, who headed up the fighter arm, began hoarding fuel and aircraft for "the big blow" – the commitment of every available fighter in the west (some 2,000 aircraft in total) against USAAF "heavies" on a single day. He hoped to shoot down 400–500 bombers for the loss of 400 fighters and, possibly, 100–150 pilots. Galland thought that such a blow would force the USAAF to halt its bombing offensive.

However, Galland's carefully husbanded force, trained in high-altitude anti-bomber tactics, was ordered by Hitler instead to support the Wehrmacht's new land offensive in the west, dubbed the "Battle of the Bulge." The campaign was launched on December 16, 1944, and the Jagdwaffe took advantage of bad weather to offer close support to the ground troops. With the skies clearing, however, losses mounted as the counteroffensive was targeted by overwhelming Allied air power. In an effort to blunt the latter, the Jagdwaffe was ordered to conduct one massive attack against the forward tactical airfields in the Low Countries and France – many occupied by Ninth Air Force P-47 groups.

Codenamed Operation *Bodenplatte*, 33 Jagdgruppen (19 of them equipped with Bf 109G/Ks) attacked bases soon after dawn on New Year's Day 1945. Close to 1,000 German fighters participated in the mission, which inflicted only minimal damage and cost the lives of 214 Luftwaffe pilots. *Bodenplatte* sounded the death knell for German fighter operations in the west.

With Soviet forces getting perilously close to Berlin, Hitler transferred much of what was left of his once-mighty Jagdwaffe eastward. The only Bf 109 Geschwader left in the west in the final weeks of the war in Europe was JG 53, which claimed its last P-47 victory on April 19, 1945.

As previously mentioned, most of the P-47s encountered by Bf 109 pilots following *Bodenplatte* were flown by Ninth Air Force fighter-bomber groups supporting the advance of Allied forces on the ground. Controlled by IX and XIX Tactical Air Commands, the 14 P-47-equipped groups that were in the vanguard of Ninth Air Force operations post-D-Day saw intensive action through to war's end. These units suffered heavily at the hands of German flak batteries, and they also endured occasional reversals when engaged by Jagdwaffe fighters. The latter, however, primarily focused their efforts against the strategic bombers of the Eighth Air Force, and in so doing they allowed the 56th FG (the sole P-47 outfit in the Eighth Air Force after November 1944) to continue to claim Bf 109 kills through to April 7, 1945.

Although neither the P-47 or the Bf 109 were the best piston-engined fighters available to the USAAF or the Luftwaffe in the final months of the war in Europe, they still played an important part in aerial combat through to VE-Day.

Assigned to the last Bf 109 Geschwader to remain in the west through to VE-Day, this well-hidden Bf 109G-14 was one of a handful of fighters kept airworthy by 12./JG 53 at Kirrlach. It was photographed in late January 1945. This unit claimed the final Thunderbolt kill to be credited to a Bf 109-equipped Gruppe on April 19, 1945. Its opponents on this date were Ninth Air Force P-47Ds.

THE COMBATANTS

AMERICAN PILOT TRAINING

While the future cream of the Jagdwaffe's fighter force was receiving a blooding in the skies over Spain in the late 1930s, across the Atlantic in the USA, the USAAC had finally recognized that it would face monumental problems in developing a tremendously expanded air arm should the war that now seemed inevitable in Europe escalate into a worldwide conflict. In early 1939, USAAC chief of staff Gen "Hap" Arnold realized that US military forces had to plan for the possibility of involvement in the European war. He and other senior officers in the USAAC duly devised a scheme that would facilitate the training of 1,200 pilots by the end of 1939, increasing to 7,000 in 1940 and 30,000 in 1941. The USAAC could not accomplish this task alone, however, so Arnold's scheme called for the establishment of civilian-operated training schools.

The latter would be responsible for the primary training phase of flight instruction, with civilian schools providing all services and facilities, bar the aircraft, but with USAAC control of the methods and manner of the instruction. In the spring of 1939, eight successful civilian pilot training school owner-operators agreed to become contractors to the USAAC to provide primary pilot training for 12,000 pilots per month. The program that Arnold recommended was to take up to 36 weeks to complete, with 12 weeks each for primary, basic and advanced pilot training (ultimately, these training sessions would be conducted in ten-week periods to save time).

By July 1939, nine civilian schools were giving primary phase flying training to USAAC Aviation Cadets. Within 12 months nine more schools were in operation, and by the end of 1940, Arnold's ambitious expansion program would be training more

FRANCIS S. GABRESKI

Born to Polish parents in Oil City, Pennsylvania, on January 28, 1919, Francis Stanley "Gabby" Gabreski was studying medicine at the University of Notre Dame when he decided to join the Army Reserve in July 1940. Enrolling in the USAAC, he graduated from flying training at Maxwell Field, Alabama, on March 14, 1941. Initially assigned to the 15th Pursuit Group's 45th Pursuit Squadron at Wheeler Field, Hawaii, Gabreski witnessed the Pearl Harbor raid on December 7, 1941. Having seen no combat flying P-40s in defense of the Hawaiian islands, he volunteered to be sent to the UK to gain combat experience with a Polish squadron – he was a fluent Polish speaker.

After spending two months in the ETO ferrying USAAF aircraft to various bases in the UK, a chance meeting with Polish Spitfire pilots in London's Embassy Club saw Gabreski temporarily assigned to No. 315 Sqn. He fitted in well at RAF Northolt and flew 11 combat and two rescue missions in Spitfire IXCs in January–February 1943.

With combat experience under his belt, Gabreski was transferred to the Thunderbolt-equipped 61st FS/56th FG at Boxted in late February. Made CO of the latter unit on June 9, 1943, "Gabby" claimed his first kill (an Fw 190) on August 24. Further claims were made in the autumn, and on November 26 he downed two Bf 110s over Germany to attain ace status. The first of an eventual 11 Bf 109s destroyed by Gabreski followed three days later.

Promoted to lieutenant colonel in January 1944, "Gabby" continued to add to his score until by mid-July he was the ETO's leading ace with 28 victories. Volunteering to lead his unit on one final mission on July 20, prior to heading home tour-expired, he was in the process of strafing a number of He 111 bombers at an airfield at Bassenheim when he flew too low in his Thunderbolt and struck the ground with its propeller. Managing to clear the airfield, Gabreski bellied the aircraft into a nearby field. He spent the rest of the war in Stalag Luft I.

Leaving the USAAF postwar, "Gabby" returned to active duty in April 1947. In June 1951 he was sent to Korea to fly F-86s with the 4th Fighter Interceptor Group, and he shot down three MiG-15s while with this unit. He then became CO of the 51st Fighter Interceptor Wing (FIW) and destroyed 3.5 more MiG-15s, taking his final tally of aerial victories in two wars to 34.5. Following a series of command appointments, Col Gabreski retired from the USAF as CO of the 52nd FIW in November 1967, whereupon he joined the Grumman Aerospace Corporation. Subsequently becoming president of the Long Island Railroad in 1978, Gabreski lived in retirement on Long Island until he passed away on January 31, 2002.

than 30,000 pilots a year. One such school was Darr Aero Tech, located some four miles southwest of Albany, New York, which by September 14, 1940 had its first class of 50 cadets conducting training flights with its 15 USAAC-supplied Stearmans.

By early 1942, the bulk of the US training program was being carried out by the Technical Training Command and Flying Training Command (renamed USAAF Training Command in 1943). By 1944, the standard USAAC program for the minimum number of flying hours required to produce a qualified pilot was 65 hours in Primary training, 70 in Basic training and 75 in Advanced training. Primary training consisted of 225 hours of ground school instruction and 65 hours of flight training to produce cadets that could fly single-engined, elementary aircraft. Most recruits had never even driven a car before, let alone flown an aircraft, but they were expected to fly solo after just six hours of tuition.

Potential pilots who reached the Primary stage arrived via Classification and Pre-Flight Training.

College Training Detachments were established by the USAAF in early 1943, and everyone entering the Aviation Cadet Program from then until war's end was assigned to one of these detachments for a period of between one and five months, depending on the scores the recruits achieved on a battery of tests administered at both Basic Training and at the College Training Detachment.

By 1942 the USAAF had four Classification and Pre-Flight Centers in Nashville (Tennessee), Maxwell Field (Alabama), San Antonio (Texas) and Santa Ana (California). Classification consisted of general education tests, 50 questions per test, multiple-choice, physiomotor tests (to measure coordination) and a 64-point physical examination. Those who did not "wash out" awaited cadet classification for pilot pre-flight training. The latter normally lasted seven to ten weeks, during which time cadets attended academic classes, marched in formation, took part in PT and drill, pistol shooting and aquatic training, where they learned ditching procedures. Cadet pilots studied armaments and gunnery, with 30 hours spent on sea and air recognition,

This flight of 61st FS/56th FG P-47Cs was photographed while on a training sortie over Suffolk on March 10, 1943. The lead aircraft, later named *Doc* (eight other Thunderbolts in the unit were also given the names of characters in Disney's *Snow White*) was flown by Capt Don Renwick. P-47C 41-6267 was assigned to 2Lt Joe Powers, who subsequently used it to claim two of his 10.5 Bf 109 kills. The third aircraft in the formation is 41-6261, which was one of the first two Thunderbolts received by the 56th FG in the UK on January 24, 1943. Bringing up the rear is 41-6325, flown by future ace 2Lt Robert Johnson. He would claim the first of his nine Bf 109s destroyed in this machine on August 19, 1943.

48 hours on codes, 24 hours on physics, 20 hours on mathematics and 18 hours on maps and charts. All who were successful moved on to the next stage of flight training. Potential pilots were now given the chance to learn to fly.

An average of 600 potential pilots attended each Primary training school, students spending 94 hours on academic work in ground school, 54 hours on military training and 60 hours in 125–225hp PT-13/17 or PT-21/22 open-cockpit biplanes or PT-19/23/26 low-wing monoplanes.

The standard primary school flight training was divided into four phases. The first was the pre-solo phase, which saw students taught the general operation of a light aircraft, proficiency in landing techniques and recovery from stalls and spins. The second phase covered a pre-solo work review and development of precision control by flying patterns such as elementary figure 8s, lazy 8s, pylon 8s and chandelles. In the third phase, students developed a high proficiency in landing approaches and landing. Finally, the fourth phase focused exclusively on aerobatics.

During this training, at least half of the flights were made with an instructor and the remainder would see the pilot flying solo. Each cadet had to make at least 175 landings. Those who soloed went on to basic flying training school, where they undertook a ten-week course. Here, a further 70 hours was flown in a 450hp BT-13/15 basic trainer (later replaced by the AT-6, because the BT was considered to be too easy to fly), 94 hours spent in ground school and 47 hours conducting military training.

In ground school, five major topics were covered; aircraft and equipment (understanding the aircraft and how everything worked, including engines and mechanical theory); navigation (preparation for cross-country flights); aircraft recognition (both "friendly" and hostile); principles of flight; and, finally, radio codes and radio communication for pilots. A link trainer was also available for use by rated pilots, and this introduced cadets to the art of instrument flying.

By the end of basic school, trainees would have learned to fly an aircraft competently. Further training taught them to pilot a warplane the USAAF way. Before the end of basic training, trainees were classified – on the basis of choice and instructors' reports – for single-engine training (fighter pilots) or twin-engine training (bomber, transport or twin-engined fighter pilots). There were two final stages in the training phase prior to a pilot reaching the front line – advanced flying training and transition flying training. Advanced flying training was a ten-week course (single-engine and twin engine), involving 70 hours flying, 60 hours ground school and 19 hours military training. Single-engine trainees flew 600hp AT-6s during this period, and also used the aircraft to undertake a course in fixed gunnery.

At the end of advanced training, the graduate was awarded the silver pilot's wings of the USAAF and given the rank of flight officer, or commissioned as a second lieutenant. Transition flying training followed, pilots learning to fly the type of aircraft they would take into combat. Fighter pilots received a five-week transition course, with single-engine pilots flying ten hours in aircraft like the P-39, P-40, P-47 or P-51. Gunnery was part of fighter transition training.

For early Thunderbolt pilot Robert Johnson, he did not get to fly his future frontline mount until he joined the 56th FG in late July 1942. His new unit had been

Vultee BT-13 Valiants await their students on the flightline at Tuskegee Army Air Field in 1942. Nicknamed the "Vibrator," the first BT-13s entered service with the USAAC in late 1939. By the time the last Valiant left the production line in 1944, 11,000+ BT-13s had been built, making it America's most produced basic trainer of World War II.

chosen to be the first in the USAAF to receive the P-47, and he vividly recalled his initial encounter with the big fighter:

> In every respect the Thunderbolt was an airplane that lived up to her name. After the BC-1 and AT-6 trainers I had flown at Kelly Field, the Thunderbolt was a giant. I had been accustomed to 600hp – beneath the P-47B's massive cowling was 2,000hp. She was big, and on the ground she wasn't very pretty. But every inch of her structure was power, a rugged and sturdy machine with all the mass of a tank.

At the conclusion of transition training, pilots reported to unit training groups, where they were welded into fighting teams. Between December 1942 and August 1945, 35,000 day-fighter crews were trained. All fighter units were supplied by the operational training unit program. Simultaneously, a replacement unit training program (90-day course) within the four domestic air forces provided replacements for overseas aircrew who had been lost in combat or rotated home for reassignment.

Six months were initially required after the formation of a cadre to complete the organization and training of a new group. By 1943, preparations to move an air unit overseas had been cut to just over four months. It normally took almost 120 days and 17 separate actions by HQ officers to move the unit to its port of embarkation.

GERMAN PILOT TRAINING

In Germany, pilot recruitment and training was strongly influenced by Prussian military tradition. Prewar, and up to the end of 1940, all future officers and NCOs alike could expect to undertake six months of basic infantry training at a *Flieger-Ersatzabteilung*. Following the completion of this induction period, all recruits were reviewed for possible advancement as possible pilots. Likely candidates were sent to a *Flug-Anwärterkompanie* (aircrew candidate company) for evaluation in a series of tests in basic aviation theory.

THEODOR WEISSENBERGER

Born on December 21, 1914 in Mühlheim-am-Main, Theodor Weissenberger had been a keen glider pilot and instructor prewar. Having been kept away from the action teaching would-be Bf 110 Zerstörer pilots for the first two years of the conflict, Oberfeldwebel Weissenberger eventually succeeded in securing a posting to 1.(Z)/JG 77 in northern Norway in the autumn of 1941. He soon proved his worth, claiming his first kill on October 23, 1941. Over subsequent months Weissenberger downed a further 22 aircraft flying the Bf 110, and also destroyed 15 locomotives, two flak installations, a radio station, a railway station on the northern Russian Murmansk line and ten large barracks.

In September 1942 he was posted to II./JG 5, which was equipped with Bf 109Es and based in Petsamo, in northern Finland. Flying with 6. Staffel, he was awarded the Knight's Cross on November 13 for 38 victories. Promoted to Staffelkapitän of 7./JG 5 on June 15, 1943, Weissenberger had increased his score to 104 by July 4. Later that same month he received Oak Leaves for his continuing success, and he became Staffelkapitän of 6./JG 5 in September.

Weissenberger became Gruppenkommandeur of II./JG 5 on April 20, 1944, and he had boosted his tally to 175 kills by May 18. That same month he took his unit south, where it became the last complete Gruppe to be added to the Defense of the Reich order of battle. On June 4 Weissenberger became Gruppenkommandeur of I./JG 5, and he led the unit with distinction on the D-Day front. He claimed 25 kills in the Normandy region in just a matter of days, including five P-47s on June 7, two more 24 hours later and three on June 12! He also claimed a trio of Typhoons and a P-51 on July 19.

With his accumulated score standing at 200, Major Weissenberger became Gruppenkommandeur of Me 262-

equipped I./JG 7 on December 1, 1944, and he was promoted to lead the Geschwader on January 15, 1945. He claimed a further eight kills (seven B-17s, including three on March 18, and a P-51) with the Messerschmitt jet fighter. By war's end, Theodor Weissenberger had flown more than 500 combat sorties and scored 208 victories. Having survived so much aerial combat, Weissenberger was killed on June 11, 1950 whilst competing in the XV Eifelrennen motor race at the Nürburgring when his BMW-engined single-seater crashed on the first lap.

With the growing demand for pilots following the commencement of World War II, the Luftwaffe's training and recruiting staff rationalized and compressed the initial stages of aircrew selection to enable trainees to embark upon the most appropriate training regime more expeditiously. The Flieger-Ersatzabteilung was now replaced by a series of *Flieger-Ausbildungsregiments*, where recruits would receive basic military training and preliminary aviation instruction. Potential pilots were then sent to undergo the standard selection process within a Flug-Anwärterkompanie, where the rest of their basic training, conducted over a period of three to four months, was completed alongside the aircrew evaluation tests.

Upon assignment to a Flug-Anwärterkompanie, the *Flugzeugführer-Anwärter* (pilot candidate) would receive instruction in basic flight theory and rudimentary aeronautics in aircraft such as the Bü 131, Ar 66C, He 72 Kadet, Go 145 and Fw 44 Stieglitz biplane trainers. Assessed for advancement throughout this phase, those candidates displaying the required aptitude were sent to Flugzeugführerschule A/B as soon as a space became available – typically two months after arriving at the Flug-Anwärterkompanie. Here, flight training proper would be undertaken.

At such schools, students underwent four principal levels of instruction, each requiring qualification for its own license, before advancing to the next stage. These licenses, earned over a period of six to nine months, gave the schools their name. The A1-Schien introduced students to basic practical flying in dual-controlled training aircraft, instructors teaching recruits how to take-off and land, recover from stalls and attain their solo flight rating. In the early stages of the war, instructors would have been assigned four trainees each, but by 1942 this number had risen to six.

At the A2-Schien, cadets were required to learn the theory of flight, including aerodynamics, meteorology, flying procedures and aviation law, as well as the practical application of aeronautical engineering, elementary navigation, wireless procedure and Morse code. In the air, they gained more flying experience on larger single-engine aircraft.

Prior to converting onto the the Bf 109, tyro day fighter pilots under training flew the Arado Ar 96. This particular machine is an Ar 96B of the Day Fighting School at Ingolstadt, and it was photographed in 1942. With more than 11,500 examples built between 1939 and 1945, the Ar 96 was the Luftwaffe's standard advanced training aircraft throughout the war. Indeed, it was used for advanced, night and instrument flying training duties with pilot training schools, fighter training wings, fighter training and replacement units and officer cadet schools.

The next level of training, known as the B1-Schien, saw pilots progress onto high-performance single- and twin-engined machines typically fitted with a retractable undercarriage – if destined to fly fighters, older types of combat aircraft such as early Bf 109s would be flown for the first time. Students would then undertake training aimed at acquiring the final B2-Schien, having accumulated 100 to 150 hours of flight time over the previous 14 to 17 months – this figure had been cut to just 40 hours accrued in a matter of weeks by war's end.

In late 1940, the Flugzeugführerschule A/B was streamlined to take into account wartime demand for pilots. A far greater emphasis would now be placed on practical flying skills from the outset, with the A2 license being dropped and that phase of the training being amalgamated into the remaining grades.

The A-license generally took three months to complete, with the B phase seeing pilots flying more advanced types. An elementary K1 Kunstflug (stunt-flying) aerobatics course was also included in the latter phase to provide all pilots with a good understanding of rudimentary evasive maneuvers (barrel rolls, loops and formation splits). This phase also allowed instructors to identify any potential fighter pilots among their students, who thereafter received more flying time than their fellow students.

Upon completion of the B2 phase, the cadet would finally be granted his *Luftwaffeflugzeugführerschein* (air force pilots' license), accompanied by the highly prized *Flugzeugführerabzeichen* (pilot's badge) – his "wings." After an average of ten to 13 months at Flugzeugführerschule A/B, he was now a fully qualified pilot.

It was at this point that new pilots were categorized for service on single- or multi-engined aircraft, with each being assigned to a specialist flying school. At the latter, he would undergo intensive training for his allotted aircraft type, with potential fighter pilots being sent directly to *Jagdfliegervorschulen* or *Waffenschule* for three to four months, where they carried out 50 hours of flying on semi-obsolescent types. For Bf 109 pilots in 1943–44, this usually meant Ar 68 and He 51 biplanes (becoming

Student pilots from fighter training Geschwader JG 102 await the signal from their instructor that will give them clearance to take-off from Wiesbaden-Erbenheim in their Bf 109G-2s and fly a training sortie. This photograph was taken in the autumn of 1943.

Bf 109G-6 COCKPIT

1. Revi C/12D reflector gunsight (later series used Revi 16B)
2. Gunsight padding
3. Ammunition counters
4. Armament switch
5. Repeater compass
6. Artificial horizon / turn and bank indicator
7. Manifold pressure gauge
8. AFN2 homing indicator (for FuG16ZY only)
9. Tumbler switch
10. Canopy jettison lever
11. Main light switch
12. Instrument panel light
13. Ignition switch
14. Start plug cleansing switch
15. Altimeter
16. Airspeed indicator
17. Tachometer
18. Propeller pitch position indicator
19. Fuel warning lamp
20. Combined coolant exit and oil intake temperature indicator
21. Starter switch
22. Fuel contents gauge
23. Undercarriage position indicator
24. Undercarriage control switch
25. Undercarriage switch
26. Undercarriage emergency release lever
27. Dual oil and fuel content gauge
28. Throttle
29. Throttle-mounted propeller pitch control thumbswitch
30. Dust filter handgrip
31. Bomb release button
32. Firing trigger
33. Control column
34. Auxiliary fuel contents indicator
35. Rudder pedal
36. Radiator cut-off handle
37. Ventilation control lever
38. Oil cooler flap control
39. Fuel cock lever
40. 20mm MG151/20 cannon breech cover
41. Radiator shutter control lever
42. FuG16ZY radio control panel
43. Drop tank fuel pipe
44. Oxygen supply indicator
45. Oxygen pressure gauge
46. Radio control panel
47. Oxygen supply
48. Fuel injection primer pump
49. Tailplane incidence indicator
50. Undercarriage emergency lowering handwheel
51. Tailplane trim adjustment wheel
52. Seat
53. Radio tuner panel

P-47D-25 THUNDERBOLT COCKPIT

1. Rudder trim tab control
2. Aileron trim tab control
3. Elevator trim tab control crank
4. Cockpit spotlight
5. Wing flap control handle
6. Landing gear control handle
7. Gun safety switch
8. Fuel selector valves
9. Supercharger control
10. Throttle
11. Microphone push-to-talk button
12. Propeller control
13. Mixture control
14. Hydraulic hand pump
15. Main switch box
16. Circuit breakers
17. Dive flap controls
18. Canopy open/close switch
19. Control switch box for constant speed propeller
20. Ammeter
21. Master battery switch
22. Ignition switch
23. Air speed indicator
24. Clock
25. Rear radar warning lamp
26. K-14A gunsight
27. Rearview mirror
28. Landing gear warning lights
29. Directional gyro turn indicator
30. Artificial horizon
31. Carburetor air temperature gauge
32. Turbo rpm gauge
33. Fuel pressure warning lights
34. Oil and fuel pressure temperature gauge
35. Defroster control lever
36. Engine primer
37. Oil temperature gauge
38. Cowl flap control lever
39. Control column
40. Rudder pedals
41. Altimeter
42. Turn and bank indicator
43. Accelerometer
44. Rate of climb indicator
45. Suction gauge
46. Engine hours gauge
47. Compass
48. Fuel warning light
49. Fuel contents gauge
50. Gun firing button
51. Manifold pressure gauge
52. Hydraulic and oxygen pressure gauges
53. Engine starter switches
54. Tachometer
55. Recognition light switches
56. Oxygen regulator
57. Flare pistol port cover
58. Crystal filter selector switch
59. Cockpit vent control
60. Tailwheel lock
61. VHF radio control box
62. Command transmitter control box
63. Identification light switches
64. IFF radio destroyer buttons
65. Command receiver control box
66. Pilot's seat

progressively rare by then), Bf 109D/Es, captured French Dewoitine D.520s and Ar 96s. By the time he was eventually posted to a frontline unit, a pilot could expect to have 200 hours of flying time under his belt.

The realities of war led the Luftwaffe to modify the final stages of its training syllabus in 1940 through the creation of *ErganzungsGruppen* (Operational Training Schools) for the teaching of tactics and further familiarization with frontline types. In the Jagdwaffe, these units were directly linked to, and controlled by, operational geschwader. Designated IV Gruppe, the intention of these units was to allow new pilots to gain precious operational experience before being hurled into combat.

By the summer of 1942, the loss of so many experienced pilots meant that there was insufficient manpower available to carry out the training function in operational squadrons, so the importance of the ErganzungsGruppen was steadily reduced. Those attached to frontline fighter units were eventually disbanded in mid 1942 and replaced by three Fighter Pools located in the three main operational areas for the Luftwaffe – in the South at Cazeaux, in France (ErganzungsJagdgruppe Süd), in the West at Mannheim, in Germany (ErganzungsJagdgruppe West), and in the East at Krakow, in Poland (ErganzungsJagdgruppe Ost).

All operational units would draw replacement crews from these pools until war's end. Although the creation of these pools reduced the number of instructors required, thus freeing up more experienced pilots for frontline service, it also effectively curtailed the operational training of new pilots in the frontline at a time when such experience was critically needed for newcomers receiving their first exposure to combat. Just as serious was the elimination of a fully crewed, but only partially trained, reserve that the ErganzungsGruppen offered to frontline units.

For those pilots destined to fly the Bf 109 in 1943–45, the trio of Erganzungs-Jagdgruppen were equipped with a varied fleet of fighters covering all major variants. There were also a handful of two-seat Bf 109G-12s on strength with these units from late 1943, although they were vastly outnumbered by conventional single-seaters.

In an effort to reduce the number of accidents befalling student pilots converting onto the Bf 109G, the RLM contracted Blohm & Voss to hastily produce a two-seat version of the "Gustav." The first examples began reaching the Luftwaffe in late 1943, and some 494 Bf 109G-12s were eventually built. Existing Bf 109G-2/4/6 airframes formed the basis for the modification, which saw an additional seat and extra glazing added behind the cockpit. With internal fuel almost halved in order to make room for the second seat, the G-12 had an endurance of just 35 minutes. This meant that the aircraft was rarely seen without a 300-liter drop tank affixed to its belly shackles.

Between January and April 1944, the Luftwaffe's day-fighter arm lost more than a thousand pilots in action, which included the core of its experienced fighter leader cadre. The training organization was hard-pressed to make good losses of this magnitude, and in a desperate attempt to shore up flagging Homeland defense units, hours were cut and courses curtailed in order to get new students expeditiously into frontline Gruppen. As many as 30 trainees (the equivalent of an entire Gruppen) per conversion course were now being lost in fatal crashes due to inexperience and a lack of flying hours in tricky types such as the Bf 109G. And those that completed their schooling were of little immediate use, other than to make up numbers.

Leutnant Heinz Knoke of 5./JG 11 recalled in his book *I Flew for the Führer* how his unit dealt with fresh-faced aviators that seemed to be arriving on a near-daily basis:

> April 28, 1944. A steady stream of new pilots arrived on posting to us during recent weeks. With the exception of a flight sergeant who came from the Eastern Front, they are all young NCOs without experience, posted to us directly upon completion of courses at training schools which are altogether inadequate for operational requirements. I myself take them up for about 120 training flights. Two veteran combat pilots in the unit also give them instruction in blind flying. In addition, they receive advanced instruction in bombing and gunnery.

One of the replacements sent to a Defense of the Reich unit at this time was 22-year-old Ernst Schröder, who recounted his impression of the Bf 109G in Marco Fernández-Sommerau's *Messerschmitt Bf 109 Recognition Manual*:

> Although the Bf 109 could fly at higher altitudes than its great rival, the Fw 190, it was a crime to have allowed its development to last so long. To train a pilot on this aircraft took longer than in the Fw 190, and time is what we did not have in 1944. The Bf 109 had a large blind spot to the rear, but in combat a fighter pilot has to observe the rear quarter five times more than the front. In the Fw 190, I could easily see my rudder, and

The Bf 109G-12 was another instance of "too little, too late" when the Luftwaffe tried to halt the decline in training standards in late 1943. After increasingly perfunctory basic training, the great majority of fighter pilots at this time transitioned straight to frontline single-seaters such as this "Gustav," its school role indicated only by the three-digit fuselage numeral.

therefore spot the danger coming from the rear. I couldn't see my rudder in the Bf 109, and the all-round visibility was equally as poor due the heavy framework that dominated the fighter's canopy. The rear-view mirror fitted to the Bf 109 was also near useless due to excessive vibration in flight.

The Messerschmitt's handling was also outmoded by 1944, and it lacked electrical equipment to activate the flaps and to effect trim adjustments – this was all done with electrics in the Fw 190. The position of the parachute beneath the pilot also caused problems, and the cockpit canopy was difficult to jettison. The pilot had to pull a lever and then lift the 50kg canopy by hand to eject it.

The best modification that could have been made to the Bf 109G from a junior pilot's perspective would have been to have moved the undercarriage outward, and to strengthen it overall. This would have cured all the problems associated with the fighter during take-offs and landings. The Bf 109 tended to swing on take-off or landing along the movement of the wing's axis. Although experienced pilots soon grew accustomed to this, and could use the propeller torque to their advantage, novices often found themselves being brutally pulled to the left, which caused countless accidents – particularly in the final 18 months of the war.

Although I never personally damaged any Messerschmitts while learning to become a fighter pilot with 3./JG 101 at Pau, in France, in early 1944, I still thought that the Bf 109G was a "Scheissbock" (shitbucket), and it was a crime that it was manufactured until 1945.

A graphic example of what could happen to the unwary when taking off or landing in the Bf 109G. Oberfeldwebel Alfred Müller of 4./JG 27 poses somewhat sheepishly beside the spectacular remains of his "Gustav" following a training accident at Fels am Wagram in June 1944. And Müller was no novice, having claimed eight victories over Allied aircraft prior to the crash. He would double his tally (which included five "heavies") prior to being killed in action on August 16, 1944.

COMBAT

P-47 THUNDERBOLT TACTICS

There was no official edict on how formations should be flown when the Eighth Air Force commenced fighter operations in the ETO, so P-47 groups experimented to find the most desirable for control and deployment against an increasingly elusive enemy.

On April 17, 1943, 56th FG CO Col "Hub" Zemke tried out a new formation, staggering the squadrons and flights so that the group was like a giant V when viewed in plan. Twelve days later, 112 P-47s of the 4th, 56th and 78th FGs flew a high altitude Rodeo over the enemy coastline, sweeping overland from Ostend to Woensdrecht. The 56th FG, led by Maj Dave Schilling, lost two Thunderbolts to enemy Fw 190s flying in pairs and firing short, well-aimed bursts, before diving away. A change in US tactics followed.

Hitherto, individual flights had gone out in close finger-fours, each shifting into string trail behind its leader at the enemy coast. This flight battle formation, advised by the RAF in Stateside training days, placed the rearmost pilot in a very vulnerable position. Squadronmates were usually unable to warn him of a surprise attack from the rear, and in such an event the enemy was ideally placed to pick off the remaining aeroplanes ahead in the line. To improve matters, Zemke staggered the two-aeroplane elements in a flight, and spread flights out in very loose formation to give better positioning for spotting attackers coming in from the rear. Pilots now had more flexibility for evasion too.

On May 18, when the three P-47 groups sortied along the Dutch coast once again, a dozen Bf 109Gs approached the 4th FG at 30,000ft after the Thunderbolts had turned for England. The German fighters came in astern and the P-47s broke around

Ex-301st FS/332nd FG P-47D-16 42-75971 is seen abandoned at Göttingen airfield shortly after VE-Day. Having been landed in error by its pilot at Axis-controlled Rome-Littorio airport on May 29, 1944 during a routine ferry flight between the Allied airfields at Foggia Main and Ramitelli, the captured Thunderbolt was subsequently flown to Germany by Luftwaffe Flight Test Center pilot Hans-Werner Lerche.

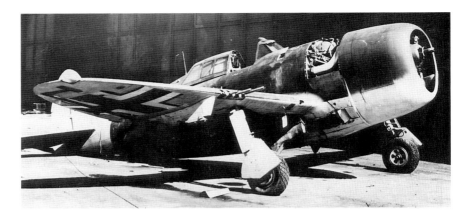

and dived on them. The Bf 109Gs dived away in accordance with Jagdwaffe standard procedure, but this was a suicidal move. The Thunderbolts turned into them with a vengeance, 1Lt Duane W. Beeson (the top ace in the 4th FG during the P-47 era) chasing Oberfeldwebel Heinz Wefes of 4./JG 54 until he baled out at 100ft for the first of his 17 victories. This was also the first Bf 109 to fall to a P-47.

The engagement on May 18 revealed the strong points of the Thunderbolt, which were exploited over and over again by USAAF pilots through to VE-Day. It had quickly become obvious to VIII Fighter Command that the P-47 was inferior to the Bf 109G and Fw 190A at altitudes up to 15,000ft, and that the German aircraft had notably better rates of climb. Indeed, according to Luftwaffe Flight Test Center pilot Hans-Werner Lerche, who extensively flew a captured P-47D-2 in late 1943, "the Thunderbolt was rather lame and sluggish near ground level, with a maximum speed of barely 310mph."

Above 15,000ft, the Thunderbolt's performance steadily improved to the point where, between 25,000ft and 30,000ft, it surpassed the Bf 109G and Fw 190A in all areas bar rate of climb and acceleration – the heavy P-47 was, after all, double the weight of either German fighter. Lerche concurred, stating "I was astonished to note how lively the Thunderbolt became at higher altitudes. Thanks to its excellent exhaust-driven turbosupercharger, this American fighter climbed to 36,000ft with ease." Under full power, the P-47 was faster than both enemy types above 15,000ft, and as much as 30mph quicker at 30,000ft. The Thunderbolt's performance at altitude, and ability to build up tremendous speeds when diving, ultimately proved to be its biggest assets in combat. USAAF bombers usually operated at heights in excess of 24,000ft, which was in the P-47's optimum performance zone.

Enemy fighters would attempt to get above the "heavies" and dive through their ranks in slashing attacks, and this suited the P-47 pilots, who would in turn try and get above the Fw 190s and Bf 109s and hunt them down as they dived on their targets.

Thanks to its weight advantage, the P-47 could soon close on a diving German fighter, even if the latter initially accelerated away from the pursuing American interceptor. Hans-Werner Lerche found that the performance of the Republic fighter when heading earthward was a revelation. "The strength of the Thunderbolt in a dive was particularly impressive. This was just as well, as it was no great dogfighter, particularly at heights below 15,000ft. It was excellent at higher altitudes, in diving attacks and when flying with maximum boost. No wonder then that the P-47s were always the decisive factor as escort fighters for bomber attacks conducted at higher altitudes."

Although acknowledging its limitations, "Hub" Zemke was also fulsome in his praise of the P-47:

A rugged beast with a sound radial engine to pull you along, it was heavy in firepower – enough to chew up an opponent at close range. It accelerated poorly and climbed not much better. But once high cruising speed was attained, the P-47 could stand up to the opposition. Strangely, the rate of roll and maneuverability were good at high speeds. At altitude, above 20,000ft, the P-47 was superior to the German fighters. In my book, you use your aircraft as advantageously as you can. In the dive, my God, the P-47 could overtake anything. Therefore, I made it policy in my group that we used the tactic of "dive and zoom." We stayed at high altitude, dived on the enemy, then zoomed back to high altitude before the next attack. To try to engage Bf 109s and Fw 190s in dogfights below 15,000ft could be suicidal – that was not playing the game our way.

Two of the 4th FG's leading aces pose for an official USAAF photograph at Debden in early 1944. Duane Beeson (left) was credited with destroying the very first Bf 109 to fall to a P-47 on May 18, 1943, and he would subsequently claim a further six "Gustavs" destroyed while flying the Thunderbolt. His final tally was 17.333 victories. Don Gentile destroyed 7.5 Bf 109s, but these all fell to him after he had swapped his P-47D for a P-51B. Gentile survived the war with a score of 21.833 kills, 4.333 of which came at the controls of a Thunderbolt.

The P-47's problems at lower altitudes were subsequently cured with the introduction of paddle-blade propellers and water injection, but until these improvements arrived in early 1944, Thunderbolt pilots were advised to avoid combats at low altitudes and slow speeds – the P-47 could turn with its more nimble German opponents provided its pilot kept his speed above 200mph. They were also told never to try to climb away from an enemy fighter unless having gained good speed in a dive. Just how poor the early P-47s were at climbing is illustrated by the fact that a Bf 109G averaged 11 minutes to climb from near ground level to 30,000ft, an Fw 190A took 14 minutes and the Thunderbolt required a full 20 minutes!

With P-47 pilots still finding their feet in combat in 1943, and hamstrung by flying less capable versions of the Thunderbolt, they found their opponents more than ready to exploit their numerous weaknesses in these early clashes over occupied Europe. 1Lt Robert S. Johnson recalled "There was no questioning the battle experience or the skill of the German pilots, nor could we find solace in the outstanding performance of the Fw 190 or Bf 109 fighters." After one of the first clashes between the 56th FG and the Jagdwaffe, Johnson noted "The Germans hit the lower squadrons hard, Me 109s and Fw 190s attacking in pairs. The Luftwaffe boys were hot. They screamed in from dead ahead, working perfectly as teams, throwing their bullets and cannon shells expertly into the evading Thunderbolts."

As losses mounted due to Jagdwaffe units seemingly always entering the battle with a height advantage, USAAF P-47 units began flying at ever-increasing altitudes.

Fighter groups would approach the enemy coastline at 30,000ft, which was well above the optimum altitude of the Fw 190A and Bf 109G. And although their presence was noted by the Gruppen scrambled to engage USAAF bombers at 20,000–25,000ft, they could often be ignored by the German pilots as they were rarely released to dive on them by over-cautious commanders. Numerous seasoned Luftwaffe aces developed an open contempt for the P-47s during this period, dubbing them the "non-intervenors." Such an attitude would come back to haunt the Jagdflieger as the year progressed and VIII Fighter Command grew more confident in its use of the Thunderbolt.

As the P-47 units accrued more experience during the bomber escort missions that they were flying over France and the Low Countries, so their toll of enemy aircraft destroyed began to steadily grow. The 56th FG's 1Lt Robert S. Johnson was among a growing band of pilots proving that the P-47 was indeed a fighter to be reckoned with when flown to its strengths. He proved this when he claimed his first Bf 109 kill (almost certainly Leutnant Werner Grupe of 12./JG 26, who was flying a Bf 109G-4) on August 19, 1943. Johnson was wingman for Capt Jerry Johnson, who had claimed two Bf 109s destroyed 48 hours earlier, and who would ultimately down eight "Gustavs" (he was also the 56th FG's first ace):

I hit the throttle, giving the P-47 her head. The moment the second Me 109 spotted me coming in, he snapped over in a sharp turn and fled to the north. Jerry was only 90 degrees to him as I swung onto his tail. I closed in rapidly to 150 yards and prepared to fire. Suddenly Jerry kicked rudder and sent a burst into the Me 109. A good boy in that Messerschmitt – he pulled into a terrific turn and kicked his plane into a spin. I rolled and dove, waiting for the Me 109 to make his first full turn. I knew just where he'd be for his second turn, and I opened fire at this spot.

Sure enough! The Messerschmitt spun right into my stream of bullets. Immediately he kicked out of the spin and dove vertically. Oh no you don't! I rolled the Jug, and from 27,000ft raced after the fleeing Me 109. The Messerschmitt seemed to crawl as the Thunderbolt fell out of the sky. I lined up directly behind the sleek fighter and squeezed the trigger. Eight heavy guns converged their fire. My second kill vanished in a blinding explosion that tore the fighter into shreds.

As the summer turned to autumn, VIII Fighter Command began to prevail in the war torn skies over Europe, although the restricted range of the P-47 still meant that heavy bombers were suffering terrible losses as the hands of the Jagdwaffe. Thunderbolt losses, however, had been drastically reduced, and the tally of German fighters being shot down was steadily growing.

Eventually, the fitting of bomb shackles to the fuselage centerline and under the wings of the P-47D allowed 75 gal and 108 gal tanks to be carried, thus boosting the fighter's endurance beyond three hours.

In early 1944, with the Eighth Air Force still very much up against it in respect to the losses its bombers were incurring at the hands of a stubborn enemy as the "heavies" broadened their campaign against targets across Germany, the way in which

VIII Fighter Command was to be used to combat the Jagdwaffe significantly changed. "Hub" Zemke recalled:

> Gen Ira Eaker (commander of the Eighth Air Force) had always told us that our first objective was to bring back the bombers and our second was to shoot down enemy aircraft. Now Lt Gen James Doolittle (who took over control of the Eighth from Eaker in January 1944) told us to pursue the enemy when and wherever we could – we were now permitted to follow him down, and no longer had to break off attacks. At lower altitudes the P-47 would have to be wary of getting into dogfights, but apparently our generals believed that there were now sufficient P-47s to warrant the risk of it keeping the pressure on the now hard-pressed Luftwaffe fighter arm. It also meant official recognition of what I had long advocated – getting way out ahead to bounce the enemy fighters before they had a chance to make their attacks on the bombers.

This change in tactics built on the successful foundations laid by the P-47 groups since the spring of 1943. The 56th FG led the way, claiming its 200th kill on January 30, and boasting 12 aces. But as the scoreboard grew, so the Jagdwaffe became more reluctant to avoid combat and unnecessary attrition at the hands of VIII Fighter Command. "As we sharpened our own ability to slash and to fight, the German aggressiveness so predominant in the early days of battle began noticeably to wane" recalled 1Lt Robert S. Johnson. "By no means do I imply that the German pilot was less dangerous an opponent – once battle was committed, however, the enemy fliers

Natural metal finish and olive drab P-47Ds and P-38s crowd the disperal at Base Air Depot 1 (better known as RAF Burtonwood) in April 1944. Behind P-47D-22 42-25862 in the foreground is P-47D-6 42-74647 LM-V of the 71st FS/ 56th FG. Note the various bombers parked off in the distance.

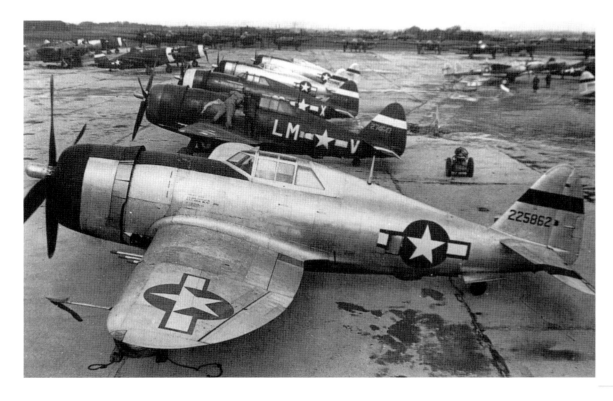

Capt Robert S. Johnson of the 61st FS/56th FG gives the camera a wave from the cockpit of his P-47D shortly after he had claimed his 24th and 25th kills (Fw 190s) on April 13, 1944. Johnson scored two more victories flying this aircraft on May 8 to take his final tally to 27 (including nine Bf 109s) – one more than ranking US World War I ace Eddie Rickenbacker.

no longer were so eager to slug it out with us in a free-for-all. Steadily, we shot down and killed many of their experienced men. At the same time, we gained constantly in experience, and in our ability to master battle situations as they erupted."

Echoing these sentiments was Maj Gen Bill Kepner, commander of VIII Fighter Command, who wrote in May 1944, "If it can be said that the P-38s struck the Luftwaffe in its vitals and the P-51s are giving it the *coup de grace*, it was the Thunderbolt that broke its back." Some of the heaviest blows to the Jagdwaffe were struck by the P-47, with a number of high-scoring Experten falling to the guns of the Republic fighter. One such pilot who was lucky to escape with his life after an encounter with Thunderbolts from the 56th FG on May 12, 1944 was Maj Günther Rall. Hospitalized for many months with wounds suffered in this clash, he would subsequently fail to add any more victories to his 275-kill tally.

Rall's Messerschmitt was one of 18 aircraft credited to the group as destroyed on this date (including five Bf 109Gs to 1Lt Bob Rankin, making him the first ETO P-47 "ace in a day"), the haul validating the introduction of the "Zemke Fan." This tactic had been devised by the CO of the 56th in response to the enemy's increasing reluctance to engage US fighters. His plan called for a P-47 formation to fly to a good visual reference point in enemy territory such as a lake, and then the four-aeroplane flights that made up the formation would fan out in different directions, with a close concentration in the center to be called in should contact be made with enemy fighters.

Eighth and Ninth Air Force P-47 groups turned their attention to supporting the D-Day landings following the Normandy invasion on June 6, 1944. Initially, however, there was little sign of Luftwaffe activity in the face of such overwhelming Allied air power, although enemy aircraft did start to appear in larger numbers in the aftermath of the invasion.

On June 10, for example, the 78th FG had no fewer than ten P-47s shot down (five falling to Bf 109Gs), but the American pilots in turn claimed seven and four damaged in a 30-minute dogfight that ended north of Argentan. Other Thunderbolt groups enjoyed mixed fortunes on this date too, as pilots were forced to dogfight with German aircraft at less than favorable altitudes close to the ground.

During this period, P-47 pilots formed the opinion that Jagdwaffe units flying Bf 109Gs had better aircraft and better aviators. However, thanks to its paddle-blade propellers and water injection, the Thunderbolt was faster in level flight and could out-turn both the Bf 109G and the Fw 190A in a high-speed climbing turn. The "bubbletop" P-47D-25, with its two-inch rudder extension, could also turn tighter than both German fighters at lower speeds too, as well as effectively "turn around its tail" while in a vertical climb without stalling out.

It was the 353rd FG's turn to suffer at the hands of a Bf 109G Gruppe on June 12, the group losing eight P-47s while making ground attacks near Dreux. Col Glenn E. Duncan's formation of 48 P-47s were bounced by "Gustavs" who attacked from out of the clouds. Targeting the rear of the Thunderbolt formation, the German pilots forced their opponents to drop their bombs and belly tanks and immediately split up into flights and elements. Those that climbed through the clouds found a high cover of Bf 109s waiting to pounce on them. The Thunderbolt pilots stayed in the area, dodging in and out of the clouds, until low fuel forced them to break for base. The 353rd FG in turn claimed six Bf 109s destroyed, with ranking ace Col Duncan being credited with three of them – at one point in this ferocious clash he called for help over the radio, stating that he had six Bf 109s "surrounded"!

Large scale encounters between Bf 109 Gruppen and both Eighth and Ninth Air Force P-47 units at medium to low altitudes would continue well into the early autumn, although as the Allies rolled back the German forces on the ground, so Jagdwaffe losses continued to mount in the air. By mid-September most fighter units had suffered such severe losses that they were ordered to return to Germany to re-equip and then commence Homeland defense missions.

The "Battle of the Bulge" in the Ardennes in December 1944 briefly saw German fighters, including numerous Bf 109G/Ks, back in the skies over Allied frontlines in larger numbers. However, their effect on the war in the west was negligible, and Thunderbolt pilots again enjoyed a brief spike in the number of victories achieved. By then the 56th FG was the only P-47 unit in the Eighth Air Force, and the group continued to escort heavy bombers as they ranged at will all over Germany. Aerial targets became harder and harder to find following the all-out effort of *Bodenplatte* on January 1, 1945, and the 56th FG claimed just 23 Bf 109s destroyed in the last four months of the war.

NEXT PAGE:
On March 8, 1944, 623 bombers from ten combat wings were sent to attack Berlin for the third time in a week. The 352nd FG was one of the fighter groups that provided withdrawal support that afternoon for the "heavies" returning from "Big B." Ten minutes after meeting the bombers, the group's 487th FS spotted three Bf 109G-6s, led by Major Klaus Mietusch of III./JG 26, performing a beam attack out of the sun on the bombers in the rear combat wing. Mietusch claimed a B-17 shot out of formation south of Zwolle-Braunschweig at 1325hrs, but he was in turn engaged by Capt Virgil K. Meroney in P-47D-5 42-8473 *Sweet Louise* and eventually shot down, giving the American his eighth victory.

P-47D-21 43-25572 *Smoocher* of the 351st FS/353rd FG is about to be towed away after crash-landing at Raydon on August 13, 1944.

All Thunderbolt aces with the 56th FG, Col "Hub" Zemke, Maj David C. Schilling, Maj "Gabby" Gabreski and Capt Fred J. Christensen stride purposefully towards a USAAF photographer at Boxted in the spring of 1944. These men claimed 25 Bf 109s destroyed between them whilst flying P-47s with the 56th FG. Zemke also downed an additional 2.5 "Gustavs" flying a P-51D during his brief time as CO of the 479th FG.

Ninth Air Force Thunderbolt units also encountered fewer and fewer enemy aircraft, with the last official Bf 109 aerial victories to fall to P-47s being credited to aircraft from XIX TAC on April 16, 1945. Conversely, the last Thunderbolts claimed shot down by Bf 109s – credited to pilots of III./JG 53 – were also Ninth Air Force aircraft, which were downed three days later.

By VE-Day, the 56th FG had scored more aerial victories than any other group in the ETO. And it had also produced the two top-scoring American fighter aces in the theater in LtCol "Gabby" Gabreski and Capt Robert S. Johnson with 28 and 27 kills, respectively. Perhaps the most outstanding tribute to this aircraft's ability to absorb punishment as well as to hand it out is the fact that all ten of the leading Thunderbolt aces (six of whom were shot down) in the ETO survived the war.

Bf 109 TACTICS

Despite being among the most skilled, and most successful, fighter pilots to take to the skies in the history of aerial warfare, the Bf 109G/K Jagdflieger defending Germany from daylight bombing raids in 1943–45 faced an impossible task. Despite using tried and tested tactics that had served them well since the Spanish Civil War, and flying an aircraft bred in combat, they were steadily outnumbered and outgunned as the war progressed.

Within weeks of the first USAAF cross-Channel raids in the early autumn of 1942, the Luftwaffe high command realized the incipient threat posed by the Eighth Air

Force's high-flying heavy bombers and their even higher (but as yet still short-ranged) fighter escorts. The rugged and hard-hitting Fw 190 was an ideal anti-bomber gun platform, but its performance degraded sharply at altitude. What was needed to supplement the Fw 190 was a machine designed expressly for the fighter role. And in late 1942 just such an aircraft was about to enter service – the Bf 109G-4. It was therefore decided that the two Jagdgeschwader in the west (JGs 2 and 26) would henceforth operate a mix of Fw 190As and Bf 109Gs.

The tactics used by the Bf 109G Gruppen from 1943 until war's end were based on the philosophy for success espoused by the "Father" of the Jagdwaffe, Werner Mölders. His mantra for aerial combat saw the emphasis placed more on fighting then flying. His combat experiences in Spain prewar had taught Mölders that the best way to achieve success against enemy aircraft was to base all tactics around the two-aircraft *Rotte*, which in turn formed the basic fighting unit for all Jagdwaffe formations. Within the pair, the Rottenführer was responsible for making the kills and his wingman (the *Katschmarek*) protected the leader's tail. The wingman did not worry about where he was flying, or what to do next – he simply had to follow his leader. He usually held position some 200 yards away from the Rottenführer, flying almost in line abreast formation. Each pilot concentrated their search of the sky inwards, so as to cover his partner's blind spot.

Two Rotten made up a *Schwarm*, flying some 300 yards apart – roughly the turning radius of a Bf 109G at combat speed. The leading Rotte typically flew to one side and slightly ahead of the other, and a Staffel formation comprised three Schwarme, either stepped up in line astern or in line abreast. The Jagdwaffe also devised the "cross-over turn" to avoid aircraft on the outside of a Schwarm becoming stragglers when the formation turned at high cruising speed in an area where contact with the enemy was likely. Each pilot held his speed going into the turn and the Rotte simply changed position in the formation during the maneuver.

The Bf 109 had always enjoyed a superior altitude performance to the fighters it had come up against since the start of World War II, so the favored tactic of Jagdflieger

Pilots from 7./JG 3 sprint for their Bf 109G-6s during an emergency scramble by the Staffel's Alarmrotte at Schiphol during the late summer of 1943. Both aircraft are parked into wind, with a vast expanse of open airfield in front of them.

Maj Günther Rall claimed 275 kills in World War II, the last of which, on May 12, 1944, was a P-47D from the 56th FG. He was then shot down by a second "Wolfpack" Thunderbolt.

This Bf 109G-6 of IV./JG 27 features an Erla Haube hood and a tall tail unit. It was photographed at Connantre, in Normandy, in the summer of 1944.

throughout the conflict was to get above their opponents and attempt to bounce them, if possible using the sun to mask their approach. After a single firing pass, the pilot would use the speed gained in his diving attack to climb back up into a position from which to perform any repeat attacks. With enemy fighters usually being slower and more maneuverable, German pilots tried to avoid turning dogfights wherever possible.

If bounced, the Rotte or Schwarm would typically turn individually to meet the attack, and if there was no time for this, they would take advantage of the direct injection system fitted to their Bf 109Gs by bunting over into a dive. The Abschwung (American "Split-S") was also used as an alternative escape route, the pilot performing a half roll pulled through into a steep dive at full throttle – this maneuver could only be done with plenty of altitude in hand, as up to 15,000ft in height would be lost.

These formations and tactics had served the Jagdwaffe well in previous conflicts, with Rottenführer having just one job to do – find and destroy the enemy. When they were found, the formation leader was the one who went in for the kill, leaving his wingmen to cover his tail. And for much of 1943, "Gustav" pilots were able to exploit these battletested tactics when engaging P-47s. However, as the number of Thunderbolts escorting the "heavies" grew, and their pilots became more experienced, the Germans found that their opponents were using these very same tactics against them. The improved P-47D, which now also boasted a long range thanks to the addition of drop tanks, was able to climb higher and dive faster than the Bf 109G. These improvements meant that "Gustav" pilots could not long pick and choose their fights at will, waiting until the escorting fighters were low on fuel before bouncing them as the Fw 190s set about the bombers.

Posted in to command II./JG 11 from the Eastern Front, Maj Günther Rall outlined the changing fortunes facing the Jagdwaffe in the west in 1943–44 in his autobiography *My Logbook*:

Over the last months the Americans have been able to steadily increase the range of their P-47s. This machine is used both to provide cover for the bomber streams, as well as to range far ahead of them, sweeping German airspace clean from tree-top height up to an altitude of 11,000 meters. Thus certain Gruppen are employed specifically against the American forward fighter screen.

Able to take a lot of punishment, the robust Fw 190s are ideally suited to attack the carefully staggered, heavily armed bomber boxes. However, the fighter's BMW radial engine dramatically loses performance at altitudes above 5,000 meters. Fighter combats over the Reich are now often being fought at altitudes between 8,000 and 11,000 meters, where the air is too thin for the BMW powerplant to deliver sufficient power output. II./JG 11 is therefore deployed as a high-altitude Gruppe equipped with Me 109s whose engines are fitted with special superchargers, so that they can concentrate quite specifically in keeping the high-flying P-47s and P-51s occupied while the Fw 190s go after the bombers.

ENGAGING THE ENEMY

All Bf 109s were fitted with reflector gunsights, which were universally known as the Revi — an abbreviation of Reflexvisier. The Bf 109B and some early versions of the C, D and E variants were equipped with the bulky Revi 3. Obsolete by 1939, this sight was replaced by the Revi C 12/C (as seen in this artwork), and later the C 12/D. The former was optimised for fixed armament only, while the C 12/D was calibrated for fixed gunnery as well as bombing. The C 12 series were simple sights with no computing aids of any kind to assist the pilot in achieving hits on his quarry. They did, however, boast a built-in dimmer to regulate reticule intensity, and this was assisted by the fitment of "sun dark" glass to reduce glare. A small auxiliary optical sight was also installed in case the C 12 suffered a malfunction.

From late 1943 until war's end, a number of Bf 109G/Ks were fitted with the new Revi 16B gunsight. Much more compact in size, pilots appreciated its smaller dimensions when sat in the cramped cockpit of the Messerschmitt fighter.

Some pilots (particularly aces) in frontline units also had telescopic sights fitted to their Bf 109s in the field, and attempted to have them harmonised with standard Revi reflector gunsights. The sights did not collimate (adjust into line-of-sight, thus allowing the Revi to be brought into play), however, and only served to identify objects that were usually beyond the pilot's clear visual range.

Finally, the Bf 109G/K was fitted with a KG 13A firing grip for operating three combinations of armament — cowling machine guns, engine-mounted cannon and underwing gondola cannon. The grip also boasted a radio actuation button and/or a rearm button for use with the MK 108 cannon if fitted. The gun-firing and radio activation function could be safely performed by the pilot using just two fingers on his right hand.

Oberstleutnant Kurt Bühligen flew more than 700 combat missions in the West, in Tunisia and in defense of the Reich. He had joined the Luftwaffe in 1936, and served throughout World War II with JG 2, ending the conflict as its Kommodore. Credited with 112 kills (all in the west), Bühligen's tally included no fewer than 24 four-engined bombers, 47 Spitfires, 13 P-38s and nine P-47s.

All of which sounds perfectly plausible in theory, but in reality – with the German fighter arm outnumbered by anything between seven-to-one and ten-to-one – it is not so easy to put into practice.

It does not take me long to realize that over Germany almost everything is different from the Eastern Front – with one exception, that here too we are faced by a sheer weight of numbers. But these numbers are now made up of pilots who have years of meticulous training in the American homeland behind them, and who have only been declared operational after 400 hours of flying. They are fresh, aggressive, well schooled in tactics and are flying superior equipment. Combats take place on the edge of the stratosphere, whereas, in complete contrast, I have scored the majority of my victories in Russia at much lower heights. Also here over the Reich every effort is being made to match the enemy strength for strength – to send up a single Rotte or Schwarm, as we did daily on the Eastern Front, would be unthinkable here. When the Americans come, the three Staffeln of the Gruppe are led into battle together – until, that is, everything explodes apart into individual dogfights.

The scenes in Germany's skies are indescribable. Nobody who has sat in a fighter aircraft and seen the thousands of condensation trails stretching from east to west like a huge great ruler being drawn across the heavens will ever be able to forget the sight. We regularly take off with belly tanks, but have to jettison these when contact is made with the enemy in order to be fully maneuverable for dogfighting. At combat rating, we have perhaps 40 minutes in which to fight, break off the engagement and then try to find a suitable place to land.

Although always outnumbered by their opponents, the Jagdwaffe had managed to hold its own for much of 1943 thanks to the experience of the pilots defending Germany, the superior equipment that they flew into battle and the aggressive tactics that they employed. However, the arrival of improved, longer-legged Thunderbolts and Mustangs in early 1944 quickly eroded any qualitative advantage previously enjoyed by the Jagdflieger. The issuing of new orders from Berlin only made the situation worse, as pilots were told to focus all their efforts on the bombers – indeed, they were expressly forbidden to engage the escort fighters. With Allied fighters now becoming more numerous, and USAAF pilots having gained more experience in combat, the gaps in the escort coverage for the "heavies" disappeared. There was now no way for the Jagdwaffe to attack bombers only.

Despite being progressively more outclassed by later versions of the Thunderbolt, the Bf 109G remained very much in the thick of the action through to war's end. While still an effective dogfighter, the "Gustav" lacked the speed necessary to initiate combat or escape from Allied fighters. Despite these serious shortcomings, an experienced pilot could use its ability to climb and turn to regain the advantage if caught by surprise. However, the majority of Bf 109G pilots by this stage of the war were far from experienced, and they proved to be easy targets.

Among the Experten to stick with the Bf 109G through to VE-Day was Oberleutnant Kurt Bühligen, who claimed 112 kills (including nine P-47s) all in the west with JG 2. Having flown the Bf 109 and the Fw 190, he was familiar with the foibles and strengths of both. The latter's propensity to flick sharply over onto one wing during certain maneuvers was well known, and this trait was routinely employed by experienced Fw 190 pilots to extricate themselves from a tight corner. The Bf 109 possessed no such inbuilt, but propitious, flaw, so many pilots, including Bühligen, fell back on a tactic of their own devising for use in an emergency.

Hauptmann Heinz Knoke served throughout much of the Defense of the Reich campaign, latterly as Gruppenkommandeur of III./JG 1. Shot down several times, he claimed five P-47s in a final tally of 33 victories.

Leutnant Günther Landt of 11./JG 53 claimed 23 kills, nine of which were P-47s. He destroyed several Thunderbolts in the final weeks of the war.

They would fly with their machine trimmed slightly tail heavy, keeping the nose down by applying constant forward pressure on the control column. In moments of crisis, the control column could be pulled back and the nose would immediately point upwards without the momentary "mushing" which could easily prove fatal.

Leutnant Heinze Knoke, who, like Bühligen, also enjoyed success against the P-47 (five kills), was another Experte who relied on his years of combat experience to stay alive when dueling with seemingly countless numbers of Thunderbolts:

> The Yanks do not leave us alone. Today they attack Münster in strength. Just when I am ready to pounce with my flight on a formation of Fortresses over the burning city, we are intercepted by dozens of P-47s diving on us from above. A wild dogfight begins. The Thunderbolt has a clumsy appearance which is belied by its high speed and maneuverability. It can still be outfought, however, by a Messerschmitt in the hands of a good pilot.
>
> At my first burst of fire a Thunderbolt ahead of me blows up, and my wingman downs a second one. That brings the entire pack of Thunderbolts down on our necks. It is all we can do to shake them off. I try every trick I know, and put on quite a display of aerobatics. Finally I get away by spiraling up in a corkscrew climb. I know that the Thunderbolt cannot duplicate this maneuver.

Following the carnage of Normandy, the constant hemorrhaging of pilots in ill-fated Homeland Defense missions and the massive losses of *Bodenplatte*, the Jagdwaffe was a spent force by early 1945. Nevertheless, Bf 109G/K units continued to fly missions through to VE-Day, occasionally inflicting losses – but always at some cost to themselves – on Ninth Air Force P-47 units conducting ground support sorties.

STATISTICS AND ANALYSIS

Between December 1942 and January 1943, 200 P-47s had been sent to Britain. Range was not something that had influenced the equipment of fighter units destined for the ETO because it was thought that operations would be similar to those undertaken by RAF fighters, where high-altitude performance seemed to be the important factor. Early USAAF fighters such as the P-39, P-40 and Allison-engined P-51A had proven unable to match the performance of RAF and German fighters in the ETO, where most combats took place at higher altitudes.

However, the P-47 was built to operate at higher altitudes thanks to the turbosupercharging of its R-2800 engine, and although it was initially slower in the climb than its contemporaries, improvements such as water injection and paddle-bladed propellers soon gave it a performance that matched the Bf 109G and Fw 190A.

In the spring of 1943, the growing strength of VIII Bomber Command increased pressure on the Jagdgeschwaderen in the west. At this time the Luftwaffe, unhappy with the relatively small numbers of bombers being shot down, revised its tactics. On December 20, German pilots began attacking bomber formations from dead ahead, or "12 o'clock level." Closing speeds of around 600mph made it difficult to keep targets in effective firing range for more than a split-second, and German pilots were always fearful of colliding with their targets. Larger attacking formations, and simultaneous attacks by fighters, rather than in trail, were now also used. While they would still use the head-on approach, the angle of attack would be from ten degrees above the horizontal – otherwise known as "12 o'clock high" – which, in experiments, was found to be more effective. As before, the best chance of knocking a bomber out of formation was to kill the pilots in the cockpit.

All told, the Thunderbolt was flown by 18 of the top 30 American aces in Europe during the war. Official figures credit the P-47 with the destruction of 4.6 enemy aircraft for each Thunderbolt lost in aerial combat during 1,934,000 flying hours, using 204,504,000 gallons of fuel.

During the first five months of 1945, Thunderbolts flew an average of 1,677 hours and dropped 541 tons of bombs per day. From D-Day to VE-Day, Thunderbolt ground-attack operations were claimed to have accounted for 86,000 railway coaches, 9,000 locomotives, 68,000 motor vehicles and 6,000 armored vehicles in Germany alone. Thunderbolt groups dropped 132,000 tons of bombs, expended more than 135 million rounds of ammunition, 60,000 rockets and several thousand gallons of Napalm. An impressive two-thirds of all Thunderbolts produced were exported to overseas combat commands, and 54 percent of these were lost to enemy action and other causes.

Late in the war, the *Tagjagd* or day fighter pilots were badly trained and hastily thrown into the battle against all odds, and only a handful survived in the lethal skies over the Third Reich. Young replacement fighter pilots who joined the *Reichsverteidigung* (Defense of the Reich) as 1944 progressed had only limited chances to survive in air combat, as they were primarily misused as "cannon fodder." In early 1944, 50 percent of all German fighter pilots were combat experienced veterans, with the remainder being replacement pilots. The majority of the latter category had only a minimum of flying experience in first-line fighters, and no combat experience at all to compensate for the heavy losses from which the Luftwaffe then severely suffered.

It was not uncommon for replacement pilots not to have flown a fully armed Bf 109G/K prior to reaching the front line. Take-offs and landings in formation were also rarely undertaken in training units, and pilots never fired the MK 108 and MG 151 cannon prior to entering combat. The tactics employed in the front line were entirely new tasks to be learned as well. All of this occurred during a period of about two months, with severe restrictions on flying time because gasoline supplies were becoming increasingly limited.

EIGHTH/NINTH AIR FORCE FIGHTER LOSSES IN THE ETO 1942–45

Aircraft	Sorties	Victories air	Victories ground	Losses
P-47	423,435	3,082	3,202	3,077
P-38	129,849	1,771	749	1,758
P-51	213,873	4,950	4,131	2,520

LEADING USAAF P-47 ACES WITH Bf 109 VICTORIES IN THE ETO

	Bf 109 kills	Overall score	Unit
LtCol Francis S. Gabreski (P-47D)	11	28 (+6.5 in F-86A/Es)	56th FG
Capt Joe H. Powers (P-47C/D)	10.5	14.5	56th FG
1Lt Robert J. Rankin (P-47D)	10	10	56th FG
Capt Robert S. Johnson (P-47C/D)	9	27	56th FG
Maj Gerald W. Johnson (P-47D)	8	16.5	56th/356th FG
Maj Leroy A. Schreiber (P-47D)	8	12	56th FG
Col Glenn E. Duncan (P-47D)	7.5	19.5	353rd FG
Col David C. Schilling (P-47C/D)	7	22.5	56th FG
Capt Duane W. Beeson (P-47C/D)	7	17.333 (5.333 in P-51Bs)	4th FG
Capt Felix D. Williamson (P-47D)	7	13	56th FG
Maj Quince L. Brown (P-47D)	7	12.333	78th FG
LtCol Kenneth W. Gallup (P-47D)	7	9	353rd FG
Maj George E. Bostwick (P-47D/M)	7	8	56th FG
Maj Walter C. Beckham (P-47D)	6	18	353rd FG
Maj Boleslaw M. Gladych (P-47D)	6	18 (8 in RAF Spitfires)	56th FG
Capt Virgil K. Meroney (P-47D)	6	9	352nd FG
Capt Frederick J. Christensen (P-47D)	5	21.5	56th FG
Capt Alwin M. Juchheim (P-47D)	5	9	78th FG

LEADING Bf 109 ACES WITH P-47 VICTORIES IN THE ETO

	P-47 kills	Overall score	Unit(s)
Oberleutnant Theodor Weissenberger	13	208	JG 5
Major Julius Meimberg	12	53	JG 53
Oberstleutnant Kurt Bühligen	9	112	JG 2
Oberfeldwebel Heinrich Bartels	9	99	JG 27
Leutnant Günther Landt	9	23	JG 53
Leutnant Alfred Hammer	8	26	JG 53
Hauptmann Walter Krupinski	7	197	JG 5/11
Oberleutnant Herbert Rollwage	6	85	JG 53
Major Klaus Mietusch	6	75	JG 26
Hauptmann Ludwig-Wilhelm Burkhardt	6	69	JG 1
Major Hermann Staiger	5	63	JG 26
Hauptmann Heinz Knoke	5	33	JG 1/11
Hauptmann Otto Meyer	5	21	JG 27

EIGHTH AIR FORCE P-47 THUNDERBOLT GROUPS

4th FG	P-47C/D	3/10/43 to 2/44	To P-51B 2/44
56th FG	P-47C/D/M	2/43 to 9/45	
78th FG	P-47C/D	1/43 to 1/45	To P-51D 1/45
352nd FG	P-47D	7/13/43 to 4/20/44	To P-51B 4/44
353rd FG	P-47D	7/43 to 11/10/44	To P-51D 11/44
355th FG	P-47D	7/43 to 3/13/44	To P-51B 3/44
356th FG	P-47D	9/43 to 11/44	To P-51D 11/44
358th FG	P-47D	12/43 to 1/44	To Ninth AF 1/2/44
359th FG	P-47D	11/43 to 5/44	To P-51B
361st FG	P-47D	12/43 to 5/44	To P-51B
495th FTG	P-47C/D	12/25/43 to 6/45	

NINTH AIR FORCE P-47 THUNDERBOLT GROUPS ON JUNE 9, 1944

IX TACTICAL AIR COMMAND	
70th FW	
48th FG	P-47D
371st FG	P-47D
71st FW	
366th FG	P-47D
368th FG	P-47D
84th FW	
50th FG	P-47D
365th FG	P-47D
404th FG	P-47D
405th FG	P-47D
XIX TACTICAL AIR COMMAND	
100th FW	
358th FG	P-47D
362nd FG	P-47D
303rd FW	
36th FG	P-47D
373rd FG	P-47D
406th FG	P-47D

AFTERMATH

THUNDERBOLTS OUTSIDE THE ETO

The P-47D was the first version of the Thunderbolt to serve with the USAAF in the Pacific, the 348th FG commencing escort missions from Brisbane, Australia in the spring of 1943. During 1944 the Thunderbolt became operational in all active theaters of war except for Alaska. P-47s served with the Mexican, Free French and Soviet forces, and in Burma, RAF and Tenth Air Force P-47Ds operated in the Arakan campaign. Some 830 P-47 Thunderbolts were supplied to the RAF, and they were operated by 16 squadrons almost entirely in the Far East. In Burma, No. 5 Sqn's P-47 fighter-bombers flew "cab-rank" patrols directed by ground visual control posts. Carrying three 500lb bombs and equipped with heavy machine guns, they created havoc among the Japanese troops and supply lines. Thunderbolts disappeared from the RAF inventory soon after VJ-Day.

Early in 1945, the introduction of the P-47N, with its increased internal fuel capacity, enabled the Thunderbolt to begin escorting B-29s to targets in the Japanese home islands. The 318th FG on Saipan was the first combat unit in the Pacific to receive N-models, commencing combat operations in spring 1945. On May 25 the 318th FG shot down 34 Japanese aircraft without loss.

From 1947 to 1952 F-47Ns saw active service with the US Air Force and Air National Guard (ANG) units. The last active USAF Thunderbolt group was the 14th FG at Dow Field, Maine, which re-equipped with F-84B Thunderjets in 1947. At least two squadrons of F-47Ns were active in Air Defense Command until 1952, and the ANG finally phased out the last of its P-47Ns for jet aircraft in 1953.

Bf 109s OUTSIDE THE ETO

During 1941 I./JG 27 was transferred to North Africa to supplement the small Luftwaffe force then operating in that area, which was still equipped with the Bf 109E-4/Trop at Ain-el-Gazala. On September 24, Leutnant Hans-Joachim Marseille claimed the destruction of five enemy aircraft, and he soon became the most celebrated German pilot in the Middle East with a total score of 158 victories, 151 of them achieved in North Africa. Marseille was killed in a flying accident in a Bf 109G on 30 September, 1942.

Early in 1942, opposed only by Hawker Hurricane IIs and Curtiss Tomahawks, JG 27 destroyed large numbers of Allied aircraft. JG 53 was also based variously in Greece, Crete and Sicily, and mainly took part in operations against Malta. Nine Gruppen equipped with the Bf 109G were operational in July 1943, and they were heavily engaged during the Allied invasion of Sicily.

On July 5, 1943, eight fighter Gruppen, including II. and III./JG 3 and III./JG 52, equipped with the Bf 109G took part in Operation *Zitadelle*, a major attempt to regain the initiative in Russia. They claimed the destruction of 432 Soviet aircraft, of which II./JG 3 destroyed 77, including 62 bombers.

In 1943 around 600 Bf 109s were built in Hungary. In addition to production for the Luftwaffe, Messerschmitt exported Bf 109s to Bulgaria, Finland, Hungary, Japan, Rumania, Slovakia, Spain, Switzerland and Yugoslavia. Postwar, in Spain Hispano built Merlin-engined Bf 109s for the Spanish air force under a license negotiated in 1942. Finland, which had received Bf 109Gs in 1943, operated "Gustavs" until 1954. The Czechoslovakian air force was equipped with DB 605-engined Avia S-99s and a far larger number of S-199 aircraft powered by Junkers Jumo 211F engines. The fledgling Israeli Air Force purchased 25 early-production aircraft from Czechoslovakia, and on May 29, 1948, an S-199 flew its first combat mission for the *Chel ha'Avir*. Czechoslovakian Bf 109s remained in service until 1957.

A Schwarm of Bf 109F-4/trops from 5./JG 27 prepares for a hurried take-off from Ain-el-Gazala, in Libya, in December 1941.

FURTHER READING

Bishop, Stan D. and Donald A. Hey, *Losses of the US 8th and 9th Air Forces* (Bishop Books, 2004)

Boiten, Theo and Martin W. Bowman, *Raiders of the Reich. Air Battle Western Europe: 1942–1945* (Airlife, 1996)

Boiten, Theo and Martin W. Bowman, *Battles With the Luftwaffe* (Janes, 2001)

Bowman, Martin W., *Great American Air Battles of World War 2* (Airlife, 1994)

Caldwell, Donald J., *JG 26 – Top Guns of the Luftwaffe* (New York, 1991)

Caldwell, Donald J., *The JG 26 War Diary Vol 2* (Grub Street, 1998)

Cora, Paul B., *Yellowjackets! The 361st FG in World War II* (Schiffer 2002)

Davis, Larry, *P-47 Thunderbolt In Action* (Squadron Signal No. 67, 1984)

Drendel, Lou, *Walk Around No 11 P-47 Thunderbolt* (Squadron Signal, 1997)

Duxford Diary 1942–45 (W. Heffer & Sons, 1945)

Fernández-Sommerau, Marco, *Messerschmitt Bf 109 Recognition Manual* (Classic Publications, 2004)

Foreman, John, *1944 – The Air War Over Europe June 1st – 30th Over the Beaches* (ARP, 1994)

Forsyth, Robert with Eddie Creek, *Luftwaffe Colours Volume 5 Section 1 Defending the Reich 1943–44* (Classic Publications, 2004)

Forsyth, Robert, *Luftwaffe Colours Volume 5 Section 3 Defending the Reich 1944-45* (Classic Publications, 2005)

Freeman, Roger A., *Osprey Aviation Elite Units 2 – 56th Fighter Group* (Osprey, 2000)

——, *USAAF Colours Volume 3 American Eagles P-47 Thunderbolt Units of the Eighth Air Force* (Classic Publications, 2002)

Green, William, *Warplanes of the Third Reich* (Doubleday, New York 1972)

Held, Werner, *Fighter! Luftwaffe Fighter Planes and Pilots* (New York, 1979)

Johnson, Air Vice Marshal J. E. "Johnnie," *Full Circle: The Story of Air Fighting* (Pan, 1964)

Johnson, Robert S., *THUNDERBOLT!* (Honoribus Press, 1973)

Knoke, Heinz, *I Flew for the Führer* (Time Life Books, 1990)

Lerche, Hans-Werner, *Luftwaffe Test Pilot* (Jane's, 1980)

McLachlan, Ian, *USAAF Fighter Stories* (Haynes Publishing, 1997)

——, *USAAF Fighter Stories – A New Selection* (Sutton Publishing, 2005)

Miller, Kent D., *Fighter Units & Pilots of the 8th Air Force* (Schiffer Military History, 2001)

Mombeek, Eric, *Defending The Reich – The History of JG 1 "Oesau"* (JAC Publications, 1992)

Morris, Danny, *Aces and Wingmen* (Neville Spearman, 1972)

O'Leary, Michael, *USAAF Fighters of World War 2* (Blandford Press, 1986)

O'Leary, Michael, *Osprey Aircraft of the Aces 31 – VIII Fighter Command at War "Long Reach"* (Osprey, 2000)

Olynyk, Frank, *Stars & Bars: A Tribute to the American Fighter Ace 1920–1973* (Grub Street, 1995)

Price, Dr Alfred, *Luftwaffe Handbook 1939–1945* (Ian Allan, 1986)

Rall, Günther, *My Logbook* (Editions TwentynineSix, 2006)

Rust, Kenn C., *The 9th Air Force in World War II* (Aero Publishers, 1967)

Scutts, Jerry, *Osprey Aircraft of the Aces 24 – P-47 Thunderbolt Aces of the Eighth Air Force* (Osprey, 1998)

Speer, Frank E., *The Debden Warbirds: The 4th FG in World War II* (Schiffer Military History, 1999)

Weal, John, *Osprey Aircraft of the Aces 29 – Bf 109F/G/K Aces of the Western Front* (Osprey, 1999)

——, *Osprey Aircraft of the Aces 68 – Bf 109 Defense of the Reich Aces* (Osprey, 2006)

——, *Osprey Aviation Elite Units 12 – Jagdgeschwader 27 'Afrika'* (Osprey, 2003)

——, *Osprey Aviation Elite Units 25 – Jagdgeschwader 53 'Pik As'* (Osprey, 2007)

Zemke, "Hub", as told to Roger A. Freeman, *Zemke's Wolfpack* (Orion, 1998)

INDEX